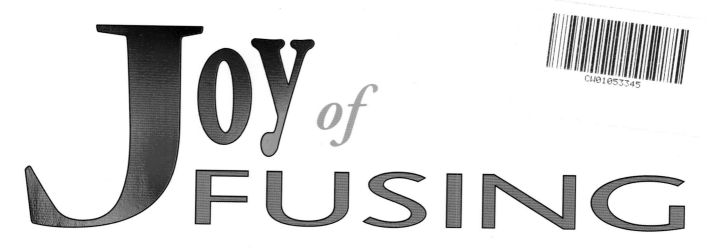

JOY of FUSING

Authors, Designers, Photography, Book Layout & Production

Randy Wardell • Carole Wardell

A Message from Randy

There is no question about it - Fusing is fun! I have tried my hand at most art glass disciplines including traditional stained glass, mosaics, torchwork (beads), etching, casting, glassblowing and fusing. I am reluctant to pick one discipline as my favorite because that is always whichever one I am engaged in at the moment that I'm asked that question.

As you might imagine, fusing has occupied most of my current art glass time as I have been researching and working on this book. Some say the immediacy of fusing is the great appeal but I think it's the dichotomy between the total control we have in the pre-fire creation stage and the letting go of control to the eccentricities of the kiln firing process. The hope for an expected outcome is heightened by the suspense of a compulsory 12 to 18 hour (or more) wait to open the kiln for the reveal. This cycle of 'hurry-up-and-wait' is both captivating and addictive.

Anyway, I would love to stay and chat but I have an idea to try something a little different in my kiln and I can't wait to see how it works out.

A Message from Carole

In 1983 I attended a workshop offered by Bullseye Glass. I was amazed as I watched the glass melt and form into a whole new artistic creation. I continued to experiment with glass fusing, even though I was kept busy in my studio creating traditional stained glass windows and doors (you can see my stained glass work in Windows of Elegance 1 & Windows of Elegance 2).

Then in 2002 we worked with glass artist Jayne Persico, to publish Innovative Adornments and Kiln Formed Bracelets. I was hooked again with glass fusing. That year I spent a week at The Studio of The Corning Museum of Glass learning many of Jayne's new glass forming and glass casting techniques. In 2003 we published Introduction to Glass Fusing with artist Petra Kaiser and I observed many more exciting ways to create fused art. I knew I had to start fusing again.

Our mission for this book is to fill in a few gaps with some mold forming techniques and a few fusing processes that we have re-conceived. We thank Jayne and Petra for getting us excited again with many glass fusing techniques, and to rediscover the 'Joy of Fusing.'

Published by

Wardell

PUBLICATIONS INC

Visit our website: www.JoyOfFusing.com for our newsletter and project support
Join our Facebook page - Joy Of Fusing • Drop us an email: hotglass@JoyOfFusing.com

Printed in Thailand by Phongwarin Printing Ltd.

Published simultaneously in Canada and USA

For distribution information contact the publisher by

Email: distribution@wardellpublications.com

Website: www.wardellpublications.com

Book Site: www.joyoffusing.com

Drapery Folds Bowl, this project was made using a single piece of Blown Antique glass (not fusible) see page 35 for full details

Cataloging in Publication Data

Wardell, Randy A, 1954-

Wardell, Carole A, 1952-

Joy of Fusing - Fusing Basics, Molds & More / co-author & co-designer, Randy Wardell, Carole Wardell; text editor, Randy Wardell; project designs & creations, Randy Wardell, Carole Wardell; photography, Randy Wardell; book layout & typography, Randy Wardell, Carole Wardell.

ISBN-13: 978-0-919985-61-2

ISBN-10: 0-919985-61-0

1. Glass manufacture--Molds. 2. Glass fusing.

I. Wardell, Randy A. (Randy Allan), 1954- II. Title.

I. Wardell, Carole A. (Carole Ann), 1952- II. Title.

Table Of Contents

The Projects

This footed vase is one of the reconceived processes that we are excited to present in this book. This sculptural process merges the charisma of fused glass with the sophistication of blown glass. Find out how it is done in the Blue Footed Vase project on page 64.

This triptych of candleholders were created in a casting mold using scrap glass shards. Find out exactly how these were made on page 70.

Glass Fusing - What Is It Exactly?

This cute little bowl is 2 layers thick. The base layer is smooth clear and the 2nd layer has a colorful stringer glass strip down the middle with more clear on either side. Coarse frit was added to the top then it was fired to FS5 - Full Fuse level (see page 28). Finally it was slumped into a small fluted ceramic bowl mold.

Glass fusing, like most art forms, can be straightforward and basic or complex and intricate depending on the artistic intention and craft expertise of the person creating the piece. Glass fusing has become established as a legitimate art form precisely because of this interpretive diversity. The discipline of oil on canvas or watercolor on paper has master artists of historic proportion and it also has genuine weekend artists who can't wait to get to their brushes and pigments. To describe the process of the painter I would say, "they must prepare a canvas, mount it on an easel, create a sketch of their subject then put paint to canvas until the work is complete". Sounds easy don't you think? Well in many ways it is, if you've studied the techniques, practiced the methods and mastered the tool skills.

To describe glass fusing in one sentence I would say, "Prepare a kiln shelf, decide on a design concept, shape and stack the art glass (all the same COE of course), place the assembly in a kiln and fire it to fuse the glass into a single art piece." Sounds easy don't you think? Well in many ways it is, if you've studied the techniques, practiced the methods and mastered the tool skills (wait, that sentence sounds familiar).

My mission for 'The Joy of Fusing' is to follow that same philosophy

- To introduce the tools, equipment and techniques for their use.
- To demonstrate and instruct the methods to manipulate the material.
- To encourage skill practice through compelling art projects.
- To inspire fun and bring joy as a result of creating art with glass.

I promise you we are going to have some fun as we experience the Joy of Fusing - so lets begin at the very beginning.

The unusual stair-step outer rim on this platter was created using multi-colored cathedral strips only - it did not have a single-piece base glass. The strips were cut to length, laid on their side and arranged on a prepared kiln shelf in this 2 layer latticework pattern. It was fired to 'Contour Fuse' level. See page 27 for this firing schedule or page 40 for complete instructions on this project.

A Succinct History of Glass and Glass Fusing

Humans have been taking advantage of glass for thousands of years. Archaeological historians have surmised that early humans used tools made from obsidian, a naturally occurring volcanic glass, as far back as 5000 BC. Man-made glass beads and decorative glass glazes on pottery have been discovered in Egypt dating to around 3000 BC. However, it wasn't until the mid-second millennium BC (1500 BC) that Mesopotamian and Egyptian craftsman learned to manipulate hot glass. They used casting and core-forming techniques (related to glass fusing) to create hollow vessels. The Phoenicians, the Greeks, the Romans, among others adopted this technique and continued to refine and create glass objects for hundreds of years.

Of particular interest to me (as a writer and publisher) the first instruction manual for glass making was published in the 7th century BC. This manual was discovered engraved on tablets in the library of the Assyrian King Ashurbanipal. I doubt very much that it became a runaway best seller.

Glass fusing fell out of use around 50 BC when, it is believed, the Phoenicians invented glassblowing. The Roman Empire quickly embraced glassblowing and encouraged its craftsmen to refine their skills. Glass making workshops were established throughout the Roman world over the next 300 years. These shops created a great variety of objects from perfume bottles, to tableware, window glass and so much more.

Fused glass techniques were largely forgotten for more than 1900 years until a group of artists in France revived a process called Pate de Verré in the late 1800's. The art glass movement was to evolving in many directions throughout the world including the contemporary glass fabrications of John LaFarge & Louis Comfort Tiffany.

By the late 1950's a few artists began to experiment by stacking and melting commercially produced sheet glass in electric pottery kilns. These early experiments lead to the birth of the style of glass fusing that we know today. A few artists continued to develop sheet glass fusing throughout the 1960's and 1970's. The movement received a much-needed boost in the early 1980's when The Bullseye Glass Company established a benchmark for fusing glass they called 'Tested Compatible Glass.' Bullseye Glass began an intense program to teach and spread the word on fusing as an art form. Today we have several manufacturers creating an assortment of products designed to make glass fusing fun and successful.

Core Formed Glass -Lentoid Flask - Egypt - 1400-1350 BC Size: 3.5" High x 3" Wide - 9 cm High x 7.5 cm Wide - 1.25" - 2.9 cm Rim Diameter. Collection of the Corning Museum of Glass, Corning, NY, bequest of Jerome Strauss (79.1.36)

Fused Glass - Tapered Cylinder - 1958-1959 AD By: Frances Stewart Higgins (American 1912-2004) Size: 9" High x 6.5" Dia. (max) - 23.5 cm x - 16.6 cm Dia. (max) Collection of the Corning Museum of Glass, Corning, NY (86.4.8)

Tools, Equipment & Safety Considerations

Artists are notorious for collecting all sorts of gadgets and contraptions to assist them in their studio and very often their favorite tool is something that was 're-purposed' from an entirely different function. Over time you will discover some unusual tools as well but for now (well for this part of the book at least) let's examine the basic list of tools that every fusing studio must have.

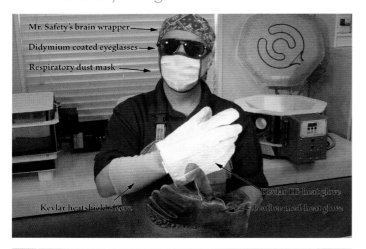

Mr. Safety's brain wrapper
Didymium coated eyeglasses
Respiratory dust mask
Kevlar heatshield sleeve
Kevlar Hi-heat glove
Leather med-heat glove

COE 90 Cathedrals
COE 90 Opals
System 96 Cathedrals
System 96 Opals
System 96 Clear Only

ProTip: Studio Storage Strategies

Studio storage is important both for convenience and safety - the single most important safety rule for all glass shops is... 'a place for everything and everything in its place'. Far too many accidents happen because something was in the way or in an unexpected place (the worst is a sheet of glass leaning against a wall or a bench). So develop a storage system that works - then use it faithfully and your studio will be a place of contentment rather than chaos.

Safety Considerations:

Let's start out with 'The Biggie' - SAFETY. Creating art with our own hands should be enjoyable and gratifying but the 'Joy of Fusing' can quickly turn tragic if we don't keep our thinking straight. Safety in the fusing studio usually boils down to common sense, for example, if it's hot don't touch it, if it's powder don't breath it, stuff like that. I am a big advocate of a tidy studio, I believe the most important safety tip of all is: 'a place for everything and everything in its place' (see ProTip below). You must own and use a few key pieces of safety equipment. They are: Safety Eyeglasses, Hi Temperature Kiln Gloves and a Respiratory Mask. Wear safety glasses whenever you're in the studio, especially when cutting & shaping glass, and using any chemicals. When looking into your hot kiln you should wear didymium coated eyeglasses. Use kiln gloves whenever you open a hot kiln and use an appropriate respiratory mask whenever you're working with anything that is or produces a powder (i.e. glass frit, resist materials & refractory products).

Designing & Pattern Making Tools:

The best designs require planning - the power is in the details. This means you will need some gear to get your ideas down on paper, things like: rulers, pencil, pen, markers, craft knife, scissors, standard drawing paper, thick card-paper (for pattern templates). I like to use my computer with illustration software to work out my designs then I print them on my laser printer. Sometimes I'll print the design directly onto thin resist shelf paper to make pre-fuse assembly easier (the laser ink burns off and does not mark the glass.

Glass Storage:

This could be as simple as a series of corrugated boxes, (sturdy pizza boxes work great for this) or you could build a custom glass rack with slots for assorted sheet sizes. I know a fuser who re-purposed an old legal sized file cabinet. She cuts her glass into manageable sizes, then sorts and stacks the glass in the drawers on edge - it's brilliant! You can easily find cube-shaped plastic containers with lids, the kind that nest-stack on each other. The 16" - 40 cm size works perfect to stack 12" - 30 cm square glass sheets on edge. I have 2 plastic storage drawer units - one for each COE - to manage my ever-expanding collection of small glass pieces (see photo at left).

Workbench or Workstation:

You'll use this for everything from preparing kiln shelves & molds to post-fuse finishing. If you are fortunate enough to have a dedicated studio space then you'll want to have your workbench adjusted to the correct height for your comfort. If you must set up a temporary workstation on a standard height table then you may want to consider building a plywood workstation-box with the surface height adjusted for you. One of my students had a workstation-box with built-in storage for tools and carrying handles. You may want to consider adding a Morton Portable Glass Shop surface to your workbench. It has pockets to catch small glass chips and the kit enables precision strip and angle cutting, plus the safety break system makes scoring and breaking more reliable (for more info see ProTip: Dancing the Jig System on page 11).

Glass Scoring & Breaking Tools:

A professional glasscutter is essential (please do not compromise on your glasscutter) it must have a carbide wheel with a self-lubricating reservoir system. I have used a Toyo Supercutter my entire career (not the same one of course but always the same brand), and they are available in several handle styles designed to fit comfortably in your hand. You'll need at least one pair of breaker-grozer pliers (two are even better) - these pliers will soon become the most versatile tool in your shop. A pair of running pliers, specifically designed to put pressure on a scored piece of glass until it breaks, can be useful but are not essential.

Grinding & Shaping Tools:

Some professional hot glass shops have a room full of power tools to cut, grind, sandblast, buff and polish glass (a.k.a., cold working). A set-up like that would be nice but my favorite machine is my glass grinder (see page 12). It is indispensable to help me fit my project during pre-fuse assembly and I use it to clean up minor edge issues after fusing. Mine is a medium duty tabletop machine with 2 diamond bits that I use all the time - medium and an extra-fine 'Fusing' bit. I use the medium bit when I need to remove a lot of material then I finish with the Fusing bit to make certain my ground edges are as smooth as possible to reduce the possibility of devitrified haze edges (learn more about this on page 19). I also have 2 small boring or pin bits that I use when I need to make small edge scallops or to get into narrow pockets. These bits can also be used to enlarge or shape drill holes.

A custom glass rack filled with a wonderful assortment of glass

Pre-fuse Assembly Supplies:

This includes everything from glass cleaning to tack gluing - all the stuff you'll need to get your masterpiece ready for the kiln. Tweezers, with bent nose, pre-fire fusing adhesive (multiple brands available), plastic wash tub - to soak and wash your glass components, a supply of fabric cloths - dishcloths, old towels or cotton t-shirts (cut into assorted sizes). Cleaners - dish soap, isopropyl alcohol (rubbing alcohol), mineral spirits (to remove marker lines and sticky residue).

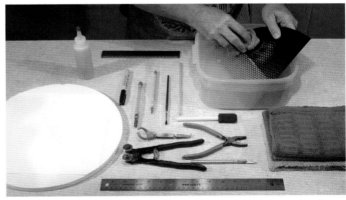

A complete array of pre-fuse assembly supplies, just add glass!

Kiln & Shelf Preparation:

Kiln wash or shelf primer (same product, different name). You will find a variety to choose from, each with it's own list of special qualities. Find one that is rated for temperatures above 1500°F - 815°C and use it universally. You'll need a 3" - 8 cm paint brush (many prefer a Bamboo Hake Brush), a putty knife (for scraping) and some extra fine sandpaper. An atomizer/sprayer is a wonderful way to apply shelf primer. I have a pump-up model that I got at a garden supply store (see page 14).

Kilns and Kiln Controllers

A fusing kiln is the most essential tool in your fusing studio and no doubt the most expensive single piece of equipment. So you'll want to choose a kiln that meets your needs now and into the future. There are dozens of fusing kiln models available in a wide range of sizes and options. I will give you a few things to think about before taking the plunge into kiln ownership.

What Do You Intend To Create?

If your focus will be on jewelry, small trays and tiles then a kiln with a firing chamber dimension of 6" to 12" - 15 to 30 cm would suffice. However if you have your heart set on larger items like bowls, platters, plates, etc., then a medium kiln from 12" to 18" - 30 to 46 cm would be a better choice. If your aspiration is to accomplish even more magnificent "objets d'art" then a professional style kiln may be the choice "du jour".

One thing I've noticed is that serious fusers usually have 2 or 3 kilns in their studio and one of them is always a medium sized kiln. That is why whenever someone asks me for advice on a first kiln I always recommend a medium sized kiln in the 15" - 38 cm diameter range. There is a lot you can do with a medium sized kiln (all the projects in this book for example) and you'll never have to feel guilty about firing a giant kiln that is only half full. As a bonus you will have the delicious anticipation of adding that 'presidential suite' kiln at a later date.

More Kiln Considerations

Shape And Vertical Depth: Size is important but you must also consider the chamber shape and vertical depth. Kilns are available in 4 basic shapes, octagon (actually 6, 7 or 8 sided), square, rectangle and oval. If you intend to make deep bowls then you must also consider the chamber depth.

Heating Elements: Kilns made specifically for glass fusing usually have heating elements positioned in the walls and in the topside (usually the lid). This duel element setup produces the even and balanced heating that is desired for successful glass fusing. Kilns with elements in the walls only can certainly be used for fusing, however the firing schedule may need to be modified with slower ramp speeds and longer soak times during the initial heat-up to balance and stabilize the heat throughout the firing chamber.

Electrical Requirement: The voltage, amperage and wiring requirement of the kiln must match the wiring and type of electrical feed in the area that you intend to install the kiln. Please consult a professional electrician to ensure your installation complies with the electrical code in your area.

Kiln Controllers: Kilns need more than a simple on and off switch. Smaller kilns have a manual dial controller with multiple power level positions and a pyrometer (hi-temp thermometer) to establish and verify the firing stages. Most medium and larger kilns have a programmed digital controller that will automatically run a selected firing schedule from room temperature to target fuse, then make a controlled cool down and soak through anneal and back to room temperature. Just turn it on to your desired fuse and let it go - you don't have to do anything. Of course you do have to enter your schedules into the controller in the beginning but after you have programmed and saved your schedules your good to go (see firing schedules on pages 26 to 28). The process for entering a firing schedule into a digital controller varies from one model to the next, but none of them are particularly difficult. The digital controller programming instructions will be included with your kiln. Note: If you can't find your kiln controller instructions look in the kiln section on the book website - www.JoyOfFusing.com, where you will find links to most kiln manufacturer's websites.

So, Which Kiln Is The Right One For You?

First you must decide what you want to create (now and into the future), do some research into what is available, ask other fusers and consult your budget. Research the various kiln models available but ultimately the right one for you comes down to a personal choice.

Glass Made For Fusing - Varieties & Classifications

The variety, types, and styles of fusing glass continues to expand. You will hear over and over again that "glass compatibility is critical" - and that is true but what does it mean? In simplest terms it means that glass with the same compatibility rating, called COE or Coefficient Of Expansion, can be heated and fused together then when properly annealed and cooled to room temperature, will be free from stress.

A Graduate Degree in COE - Not Required

Here's all you need to know. When glass is heated it expands and when it cools it contracts. The problem is, not all glass does this by the same amount or at the same rate throughout the fuse firing cycle. Think of it this way, if two pieces of non-compatible glass were stacked and heated they would expand and fuse to form one glass piece. Then as this fused piece cools one of the glass layers will shrink more than the other, creating stress as it attempts to force the other piece to contract as well. But it can't contract the same amount, it's non-compatible remember, so it will bend until it can't bend anymore and that stress will eventually lead to catastrophic failure!

Fortunately 'certified fusible' glass is readily available. Fusible glass is tested by the manufacturer and is assigned a 'COE' number. All you have to do is make sure all components in your piece are certified fusible and have the same COE rating. That includes the glass, the stringers, the frit, the dichroic, and any precut shapes. Whatever will be fused together must be compatible! That's it - that's all you need to know about COE.

Certified Fusible Categories

You will find 4 major COE categories of fusible glass, they are: COE 104 (used primarily for flame working), COE 82 (compatible with standard float glass), plus the 2 most popular choices for fusing, COE 90 and COE 96. Some studios take the decision to use one COE exclusively while other artists stock and use both COE 90 and COE 96 in their studio. If you decide to keep both, you must be diligent to mark each piece and component clearly and store them separately (see Glass Storage on page 6) because if you get COE 90 & COE 96 mixed up in a single project you will discover what 'non-compatible' really means.

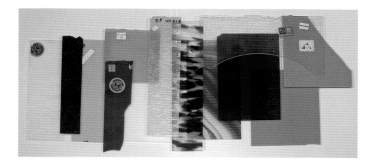

Glass Varieties, Forms & Shapes:

The most common form of fusible glass is sheet, sold in a wide variety of colors, textures and surface coatings. You will find clear glass (no color), cathedral glass (transparent colors), and opalescent glass (translucent colors). Some may have an iridescent surface coating (rainbow-like) or a dichroic coating with its distinctive and captivating intensity. In addition to sheets you will find fusible stringers (spaghetti); noodles (linguine) shards (paper thin glass chips) frit (crushed glass sorted from powder to extra-coarse) and billets (solid glass bricks). Plus precut shapes like hearts, leaves, butterflies, zigzags, stars, holiday designs, and so much more.

One Final Word About Certified Fusible

Glass manufactured for fusing has been tested to ensure the COE is correct but that is not the only difference between certified fusing glass and traditional stained glass. Fusing glass has been specially formulated to resist devitrification and this is a big advantage. In the past devitrification was a major headache for fusers. We tweaked our schedules to drive our firings through the devit temperature zones as quickly as possible and we would regularly spray a clear overglaze on our work, especially when we were using an opal glass or one we knew had devit issues. Of course we still encounter some devit periodically but it is rare and we can thank the glass manufacturers for making our task easier and less frustrating.

Glass Cutting - Scoring and Breaking

It is possible to create a fused glass piece without having to cut or shape any glass but for me the thrill is in the flexibility that comes when I am sculpting the glass to fit my design, rather than the other way around. That's when the artistic process is in full stride and I find myself lost in the creative zone. Scoring and breaking glass is not difficult but I know from teaching hundreds of first timers that the pathway to success is through a professional quality glasscutter (see page 7).

Let's review 3 basic safety rules.

1. Wear safety glasses whenever scoring, breaking, shaping, or grinding glass.

2. Never pick up or hold larger glass sheets in a horizontal (flat) position.

3. Never run your hand along a cut glass edge (may seem obvious but it will happen)

Just a few more things before you make your first score. Practice on some clear glass that has a smooth surface. Start with shorter length scores, 6" - 15 cm and slice off a piece that is at least 2" - 5 cm wide.

Making the Score

First, it is easier to score glass by pushing the cutter away from you rather than by pulling it. Second draw a line across the glass where you will score, to give you something to follow.

Grip the cutter in your tool hand and place the cutter wheel on the edge of the glass that is closest to you. Place the thumb of your other (guide) hand behind the cutter head to prevent it from rolling back off the glass edge (see 2nd photo).

Now press down on the cutter with a firm and steady pressure then use the thumb of your guide hand to push the cutter across the glass. Score slow and steady all the way across the glass and let the cutter wheel roll gently off the far edge. (see 3rd photo).

You should hear a distinctive 'scritch' sound as the cutter wheel scores the surface and you will feel a 'resistance' as it rolls along. Too much pressure down onto the cutter and it will be difficult to push it across the glass, too little pressure produces almost no resistance and the score will not be successful.

Breaking Out The Score:

Always start the break at one end of the score line (the end where the score finished is often easier) and allow it to run along the score to the other side.

Breaking with Hands Only: Form both hands into a fist and place the glass between your thumbs and index fingers with the score line between your thumbs (see 3rd and 4th photos). Hold the glass firmly and begin by pulling outward then apply a quick even snap by spreading your thumbs apart, rolling on your knuckles. The glass should break as your hands impulsively move apart.

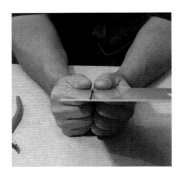

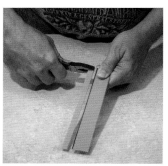
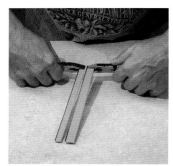

Using Breaker Grozer Pliers: Use these special pliers to grasp small pieces or narrow strips (flat jaw on top) then run the score by pulling out then snap down. If both sides are narrow use 2 pair of breaker grozer pliers (photos on previous page).

Breaking with Running Pliers: Locate the guide mark on the top jaw and align it with your score then grasp the glass about 3/8" - 1 cm in from the edge. Gently squeeze the pliers until the break runs along the score line. If the break travels only part way, move the breaking pliers to the opposite side and repeat.

ProTip: The Song of the Glass Cutter

To my ear the distinctive sound that a cutter wheel makes is 'scri-iiiiiiiiiiii-tch' (hold the 'i' for as long as the score takes). It's a satisfying sound but don't rely on it too much because it changes from one glass to the next. Sometimes it's intermittent (especially in multi-colored glass) and sometimes it's not there at all. A better indicator for a perfect score is to be aware of the resistance as the wheel bites into the surface of the glass. If the resistance is heavy let up a little on the pressure, if the resistance is slight put a little more weight on it. Learn to recognize the ideal resistance then adjust on the fly - that's the secret behind a precision score.

Breaking with the Morton Safety Break: Place the score over the button about 2" - 5 cm in from the glass edge. Now place the bar on the glass, centered over the button and aligned with the score. Press down with a firm but gentle pressure. If the score doesn't break right away, move the glass along keeping the score over the button and press down again, repeat moving and pressing until the score breaks.

Squares, Circles and Strips - Oh My!

Fusing loves geometric shapes. I would guess that 90% of fused glass pieces start out with a base glass shape that is a circle, a square, or a rectangle. So it stands to reason that you must find a way to cut these shapes accurately.

Circles: I have 2 circle scoring devices that I use regularly. One is a traditional model with a cutter head on a swing arm that spins on a suction cup fulcrum (see 4th photo this page). It scores circles from 6" to 24" - 15 to 60 cm diameter. The other device is the 'Circle & Border System' by Morton that scores circles from 4" to 14" - 10 to 35 cm diameter (see ProTip below).

Squares, Rectangles & Strips: A simple but effective tool for making all of these shapes is a glass square. You definitely need a glass square (perhaps even a large and small square) in your tool drawer.

ProTip: Dancing the Jig System

For me the most versatile tool in my studio is my jig cutting system (I use the Morton System but there are others available). Simply position and lock the cutter guides onto the grid surface to make scores that are perfectly aligned to 90°, 60°, 45° or any other angle you desire. The heart of the system is it's ability to quickly score strips of any width, each one exactly the same as the last one. Then these strips can be segmented into squares, diamonds, triangles, trapezoids, pentagons, hexagons, octagons, etc. and once again each one will be a clone of the previous one. See this tool in action on page 39.

The 'Circle & Border System' (also by Morton) is an invaluable accessory for making perfect disk-circles from 2" to 14" - 5 to 35 cm diameter but the genius of this tool is the way it makes circle border segments from glass strips, reducing cut-away scrap glass. I use it to cut narrow 'rim-wraps' that I add to the perimeter of my plates (see Craquel Bowl on Pg 82).

Power Tools with Diamonds - Shaping Tactics

Aglass cutter and breaker grozer pliers can do a lot but there will be times when you'll need some additional assistance to refine a shape or pull off an intricate design. These tasks call for special measures and by 'special' - I mean power tools with diamonds!

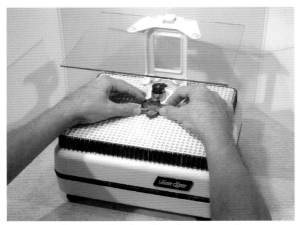

Glass grinder fitted with a Fusing bit

Diamond coated wire-hoop blade - Ringsaw

Variable speed electric drill with a core bit

Diamonds are a Fusers Best Friend

Diamond tools are available to cut glass, drill glass, grind glass and polish glass. The list of tools is extensive and well beyond the scope of this book. Instead we'll take a brief look at three general categories and consider what these machines can do for fusing artists.

Diamonds for Grinding: My trusty old glass grinder is indispensable in my studio and I have 2 diamond bits that I use all the time - medium grit and an extra-fine 'Fusing' bit. I use the medium bit when I need to remove a lot of material then I finish the edge with the Fusing bit to reduce murky edge syndrome by making certain my ground edges are as smooth as possible (see pg 19). I also have 2 pin bits, 1/4" - 6.4 mm and 1/8" - 3.2 mm that I use for fine work, especially on jewelry pieces. I can also use them to enlarge or reshape drill holes.

Diamonds for Cutting: Diamond blade saw types used for fusing include ring saws, table saws and band saws. All of these are 'wet' saws meaning the blade is lubricated with water to keep the blade cool and flush out the glass-dust. The ring saw is basically a wire-hoop that is coated all around with diamond grit and that means it can saw through glass in every direction (push, pull and side-to-side). This is a very versatile machine that I use regularly (see photo middle left). The table saw cuts straight lines only and is particularly efficient for making pattern bar slices or when strip cutting a full-fuse blank to create phase-shift patterns. The band saw has a narrow flat blade with diamond grit on the leading edge and that means they cut in the push direction only.

Diamonds for Drilling: There are 2 types of diamond drill bits used to make holes in glass, solid pin bits and hollow-core tube bits. A hollow core bit grinds a ring into the glass leaving a disk shaped core while a solid pin bit grinds a hole into the glass that is the same diameter as the bit. Pin bits are available from 1/32" to 1/4" - 1 mm to 6.5 mm while hollow-core tube bits are from 3/16" to 2"- 5 mm to 5 cm.

Diamond bits must be cooled with water as they are drilling. I use a shallow plastic kitchen container with a piece of glass that I cut to fit in the bottom. I set the piece that I need to drill on that glass then fill the pan with enough water to submerge the glass to be drilled by 3/16" - 5 mm underwater.

Then I use my variable speed rotary tool (set at medium speed) for the smaller pin bits or an ordinary variable speed electric drill (set at full speed) for the larger core bits. Be patient and let the bit do the work, pushing harder doesn't make the hole go faster it just increases friction and heat and that will end up destroying the bit.

Forming Molds & Shaping Methods

Ceramic and stainless steel are the most common type of mold but there are many additional materials that can be used.

Ceramic: Clay slumping molds are available in a wide variety of shapes and sizes to form plates, bowls, dishes, platters and more. Ceramic molds must be coated with a glass release such as primer or boron nitride (see page 14 & 15). The majority of the projects in this book were formed on ceramic molds.

Stainless Steel: You will find a great variety of stainless steel molds for glass forming. These molds also need to be coated with a release agent and while you can use a ceramic primer I prefer to use the spray-on boron nitride (see page 15).

Fiberboard: Alumina Silica fiberboard is a rigid board, available from 1" to 2" - 25 to 50 mm thick. This material has a textured surface (can be smoothed) and is very easy to cut, carve and shape to make unique slump & drape molds, casting dams, kiln shelves, and so much more. In fact this material is so versatile that Wardell Publications has three books with extensive information and projects featuring Kaiser-Lee Board (a brand of fiberboard). These books are: *Introduction to Glass Fusing, Fuse It - A Continuing Journey in Kiln Worked Glass and Glass Forming with the Mold Block System*, all by Petra Kaiser. Visit JoyOfFusing.com for more information on these books.

Fiber Blanket, Fiber Paper, Fiber Cloth: Fiber blanket is fluffier than fiber paper, available from 1/4" to 1" - 7 to 25 mm. It can be cut, folded, stacked and formed into many shapes for molding glass. Fiber rope is the same material but woven into a twisted cord-style rope from 1/4" to 3/4" - 6 to 25 mm thick. All of these fiber products can be used in their flexible form but when you add fiber rigidizer the possibilities skyrocket. You could design a custom mold using any combination then harden your construction with rigidizer to make a personal glass-shaping mold (these molds can last up to 10 firings or more if your careful).

Castable Refractory Cement: Castable products offer another way to create custom shaping molds. This cement is mixed with water and it can be applied over an existing model or it can be hand-formed. Castable refractory forms typically last from 2 to 5 firings but some newly developed compounds are promising a longer useful life.

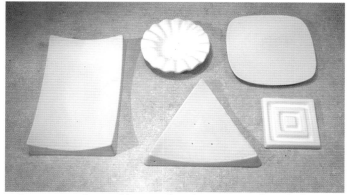

Ceramic or clay molds coated with primer and ready for use

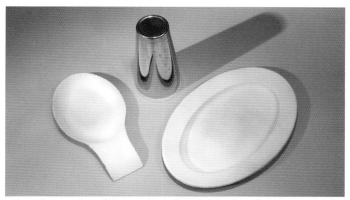

Stainless steel molds, two have been coated with boron nitride

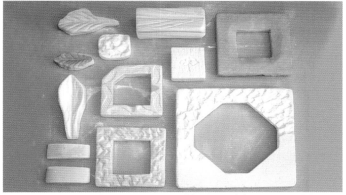

A selection of alumina silica fiberboard forming molds

Fiber blanket, fiber paper, thin resist paper

Glass Release Methods & Strategies

Re-coating a kiln shelf by painting with shelf primer

Coating a ceramic mold using a pump up garden sprayer

Placing a sheet of thin resist paper on the kiln shelf

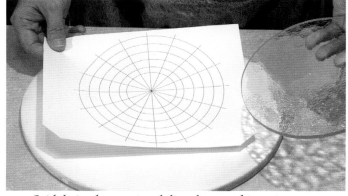

Grid design laser printed directly onto thin resist paper

When glass is heated to fuse temperature it will stick to almost anything that doesn't burn. That's why we need a barrier between the hot glass and our kiln shelves or molds. We call this category of items 'Glass Release Materials'.

Shelf Primer & Kiln Wash: The name for this product is interchangeable. In general, primers and washes are powder-type resists that are mixed with water and used to coat kiln shelves, kiln floors and shaping molds. The mixing proportions are usually 1 part powder with 4 parts water (follow product directions) - then apply 3 or 4 coats with a paintbrush. My favorite applicator is a pump-up sprayer that I purchased at a garden supply (it requires a slightly thinner mix). I spray 4 or 5 coats, allowing 5 minutes dry time between coats and that gives me an even and smooth cover every time. I always dry my shelves and molds in a 500°F - 260°C kiln for 20 minutes to cure and harden the primer. There are subtle differences between brands so do some checking before purchasing. Some primers withstand higher temperatures but may require frequent reapplication others are created for lower temperatures but they hold up for several firings before needing a re-coat. By the way, you don't always have to apply primers in liquid form, sifting primer onto a shelf works as well and you can use a stick or a comb to create textures in the powder that will be imprinted into your glass (use a respirator whenever sifting any powders).

Thin Resist Papers: This is my favorite type of separator. I place a sheet of thin resist paper under almost all fuse firings, except when I am using fiber paper or a mold. Thin resist paper offers many advantages. It is ready to go immediately, it has a silky smooth surface that leaves the bottom surface smooth and it never sticks to the glass. I also find that I get three times as many firings from my shelf primer before I have to re-coat. Sometimes I draw my design directly on the paper as a guide for assembly or if I am creating something smaller than 8" - 20 cm I cut the paper to standard letter size and run it through my laser printer (see the spider web grid in the photo). I don't normally use thin resist paper when shape firing over a mold. I find the paper has a tendency to wrinkle under the glass during slumping and that creates wrinkle lines on the bottom of my pieces (and I have enough of those on my forehead).

Boron Nitride: Originally developed for industrial metal and glass casting this product has been embraced for fusing. It is available as a powder to be mixed with water or as a liquid for brush painting but my favorite way to use it is in spray can form. I use it for all my stainless steel molds and I have started to convert some of my ceramic molds, especially my casting molds. However, once you use boron nitride on a ceramic mold you can't go back to a ceramic primer because it will not stick. New molds need 2 coats but after that, one quick coat is all it needs. I like to cure-fire new mold applications in my kiln at 250°F - 120°C for 25 minutes (I try to gang 3 or 4 molds at once if I can). This hardens the surface and cuts down on damage when I'm preparing a slump or casting project. After each use I sweep the mold with a kitchen brush (veggie brush) to remove any debris then I spray a quick touch-up coat of boron nitride. After 4 or 5 uses or if the coating starts to flake I'll submerge the mold in water and scrub it clean with a stiff brush, then coat it as if it were a new mold.

Fiber Paper and Fiber Cloth: Fiber Paper resist is available in 1/16" & 1/8" - 1.6 & 3.2 mm thicknesses. It is soft and flexible with a rough textured side and a slightly smoother side. Use it to add texture, especially when fusing design side down items. You can also use it to make shallow molds (see projects on pages 58, 60 & 62) or cutout shapes and use it to form frit components (see projects on pages 78 & 80). If you're careful you can get multiple firings but after it has been fired once it is easily damaged.

Fiber Cloth looks and feels like a polyester towel but it can be fired to fuse temperatures and resists sticking to glass. It is available in several pattern styles such as canvas & herringbone and that texture will transfer to your glass. If you remove it carefully after firing you can get multiple uses from the same piece.

Iridescents and Dichroics: These may not be considered resist materials in the strictest sense but they do act as a separator between the glass and the shelf in certain circumstances. The most common application is to use an iridized base glass, with the iridized side down toward the shelf or mold (you can do the same with dichroic). The coating will not stick and as a bonus, firing it face down against the shelf seems to intensify the luster even more. I do not recommend firing either of these directly on an untreated shelf or mold.

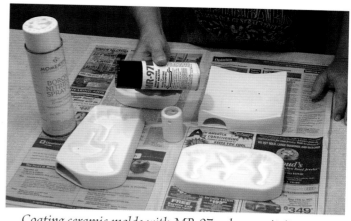

Coating ceramic molds with MR-97, a boron nitrite spray

First coat of boron nitrite spray on a stainless steel tray mold

Fiber paper shapes and a piece of fiber cloth

Iridized fired down will intensify the shimmer of the iridescence

Record Keeping - Thanks For The Memories

A famous quote by the Spanish philosopher George Santayana, goes like this "Those who cannot remember the past are condemned to repeat it." (- Life of Reason, circa, 1905). Truer words have never been spoken, particularly as it applies to glass fusing. There are times when we would love to repeat a perfect firing outcome or an unanticipated but amazing effect. There are other times when we encounter a disappointing result that we would like to avoid in the future. This is where record keeping plays an important role.

You will be amazed how easy it is to forget exactly which colors, textures and styles of glass were used, how many layers and what order they were stacked - all of these have an effect on the outcome of your piece. You may need to recall what type of kiln shelf you used, the type and brand of the release, details about the mold or other shaping material, a new process or color, or whatever you are trying.

If you're still testing your kiln you may want to record the exact position of the piece within the kiln. Of course you'll need to record the firing schedule, from ramp up speed to soak times, the final 'target' temperature, the anneal temp-soak routine and the cool down rate.

Throw Another Log on the Firing

Get into the habit of filling out a 'Project Log' for each and every firing - make copies of the blank log on the next page (for your personal use only please). It only takes a few minutes and I promise that it will prove to be an invaluable reference. I like to fill mine out as soon as I have completed my pre-fuse assembly and before I load the kiln. The materials I used are still fresh in my mind and there is another bonus - making a list of the glass and components forces me to reconsider my overall project plan and double-check the possibilities. I still have the opportunity to tweak my design or make a change before I have committed my piece to the fire.

Be sure to visit the books website www.JoyOfFusing.com to download a free PDF copy of the Project Log that is on the next page or better yet pick up one of our pre-printed multi-sheet 'Log Pads' available where you bought this book.

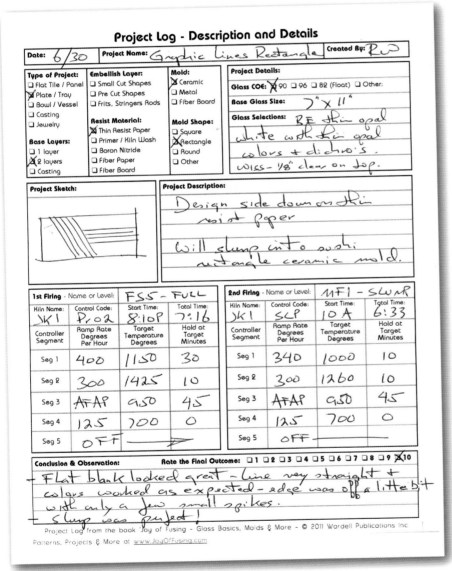

This completed Project Log is the actual log sheet I did while I was creating my project 'Crossroads Tray' described on page 72. Notice the Project Name at the top was a generic 'Graphic Lines Rectangle'. I did the sketch after the piece was completed, it may seem like an unnecessary step but is a real help later on when I'm trying to quickly identify which log belongs to what piece.

Project Log - Description and Details

Date:	Project Name:	Created By:

Type of Project:
- ❑ Flat Tile / Panel
- ❑ Plate / Tray
- ❑ Bowl / Vessel
- ❑ Casting
- ❑ Jewelry

Base Layers:
- ❑ 1 layer
- ❑ 2 layers
- ❑ Casting

Embellish Layer:
- ❑ Small Cut Shapes
- ❑ Pre Cut Shapes
- ❑ Frit Stringers Rods

Resist Material:
- ❑ Thin Resist Paper
- ❑ Primer / Kiln Wash
- ❑ Boron Nitride
- ❑ Fiber Paper
- ❑ Fiber Board

Mold:
- ❑ Ceramic
- ❑ Metal
- ❑ Fiber Board

Mold Shape:
- ❑ Square
- ❑ Rectangle
- ❑ Round
- ❑ Other

Project Details:

Glass COE: ❑ 90 ❑ 96 ❑ 82 (Float) ❑ Other:

Base Glass Size:

Glass Selections:

Project Sketch:

Project Description:

1st Firing - Name or Level:

Kiln Name:	Control Code:	Start Time:	Total Time:

Controller Segment	Ramp Rate Degrees Per Hour	Target Temperature Degrees	Hold at Target Minutes
Segment 1			
Segment 2			
Segment 3			
Segment 4			
Segment 5			

2nd Firing - Name or Level:

Kiln Name:	Control Code:	Start Time:	Total Time:

Controller Segment	Ramp Rate Degrees Per Hour	Target Temperature Degrees	Hold at Target Minutes
Segment 1			
Segment 2			
Segment 3			
Segment 4			
Segment 5			

Conclusion & Observation: **Rate the Final Outcome:** ❑ 1 ❑ 2 ❑ 3 ❑ 4 ❑ 5 ❑ 6 ❑ 7 ❑ 8 ❑ 9 ❑ 10

The Fusing Process from Seed to Fruit

Let me take you on a creative journey as I think about and make decisions for a new fusing project. Sometimes a design idea sprouts from a combination of glass or colors or components that I want to use. Then I think about a process that I may want to try - perhaps a design-side down project or a way to display it - mounted on a wall. Other times I'll choose the item I want to make, like a bowl then I'll sketch some design ideas for that item. For this example, I have a ceramic mold with a square outside shape that gently sweeps down to a circular inside base (see photo) and I would like to create a design for that mold.

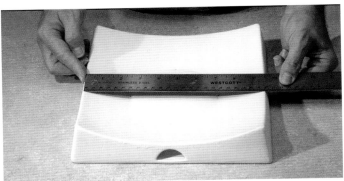
Measure the mold to find the best size to make the flat-blank

6 orange rods slumped over a wave mold for design components

A series of design concept sketches using the wave shaped rods

A Design Is Born

The mold is 9 1/2" - 24 cm across so if I make my plate 9" - 23 cm square that will give me an allowance of 1/4" - 5 mm on all sides. Now I need to come up with a design and there are thousands of ways to create a fused glass design (you'll find several ideas in this book). A design kernel could spring from something you found or purchased. For example the last time I was at my local fusing supply store I picked up some intense orange opal rods that are 3/16" - 5 mm diameter and 16" - 40 cm long. I already had a funky wave mold with 4 valleys & 3 peaks so I decided to cut 3 orange rods in half then use that mold to slump the rods and create 6 wavy lines (see photo).

These rods are relatively thin and that means I can heat the kiln quickly to the slump temperature (see Ramp Rate on page 23) then simply turn the kiln off and allow it cool on it's own with the lid closed. These smaller component pieces will be more fully annealed later when they are fused into a larger work. Here is the firing schedule I used for the rod slump.

SCS - Small Component Shaping Schedule				
Segment Description	Segment Number	Ramp Rate Per Hour	Final Target Temp °F-°C	Hold-Soak Minutes
Intention Heat Target Soak	1	900°F - 495°C	1245°F - 675°C	10
Power-off Cool to Room Temp	2	0000 Kiln Off	75°F - 25°C Room Temp	Do Not Open Kiln

What Do We Know So Far?

I know the mold I'll use, I know the base size and I know that I want to use some of these wavy rods that I created. I decide to make a few sketches to see what turns up. After a few rough drafts I settled on a narrow outside border and I think I like the wavy lines better when they are parallel to one another and 3 seems to be the right quantity for the size of my bowl, so I'll go with the sketch at bottom right.

Choosing the Glass

I'll use a thin clear for the base (bottom layer) to hold the components together during the fuse firing. I have an opal orange that is a shade lighter than my rods that I'll use to make a 1/2" - 13 mm outside border. I also have a sheet of white opal with orange, red & yellow fractures and black streamers that I'll use as the inside field. I think I'll put this glass 'fracture side' down to subdue the design a little.

Cut the Glass

The simple geometric shapes for this bowl design can be created easily with a few measurements and an L-square or if you have a Morton Portable Workshop this would be a perfect opportunity to use it. I measured and cut one 9" - 23 cm square from thin 1/16" - 1.6 mm clear glass for the base. I could have used standard thick 1/8" - 3 mm clear glass but I wanted to keep my bowl as light-weight as possible.

Now I'll make the 2nd layer. I cut four 1/2" - 15 mm strips from the orange opal then I measured and trimmed them to fit the base glass using a 45° corner angle. I could used a square butt joint by cutting each strip 8 1/2" - 21.5 cm long then place them around the edge using a pinwheel pattern. Next I cut an 8" - 20 cm square, from the fracture & streamer on white glass, to fit inside the border pieces.

Scoring and breaking the clear base glass using an L-square

Preliminary Assembly

I have the main glass components cut, so I arrange them on my bench according to my original design plan. If I had created a full-size assembly drawing I would lay my cut pieces on that. I carefully scrutinize my glass & color selections. It's amazing how often I find a color or texture that I thought would be perfect but just doesn't work. So I try something else until I like what I see. Remember that some colors change in the kiln so if color is critical to your design you really should test fire your glass (see Testing... Testing... on page 31) then if necessary make an allowance for any color shifts when planning your design.

Next I check the pieces to confirm they fit together accurately, keeping in mind that one of the perks of fusing is the fit doesn't have to be perfect. Even so I find some strategic grinding and shaping is required to ensure my lines are straight and the design is true.

Scoring narrow border strips using the portable jig system

Murky Edge Caused by Grinding

On occasion you may notice a murky discoloration or shadow along an edge that was ground. This murky shadow is more noticeable along the edge of darker glass especially when fused to a lighter color. It seems the rough-ground edge traps thousands of micro-bubbles that show up as a stain. I have found using an extra fine 'Fusing' bit in my grinder can minimize the occurrence of this murky edge. I start with a standard medium-grit bit to remove most of the material then I switch to the Fusing bit to make certain my ground edges are as smooth as possible. Then I make sure all grinder residue has been cleaned off.

Preliminary design assembly to check the fit and color choices

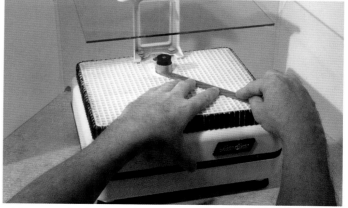
Adjusting the fit using the extra fine 'Fusing' bit in my grinder

ProTip: Gaps & Spaces as Design Elements

Gaps left between adjacent pieces can open even more due to the tendency of glass to retract when heated, especially when the assembly is less than 2 full layers thick. However, gaps are not always bad, in fact they can be embraced as a design technique. For example instead of running long strips around an edge to create a continuous border wrap, divide these strips into equal shorter lengths and allow the gaps to exist and open up to reveal the color underneath. If the gap pattern is consistent the viewer sees it as part of the planned design. It's only when gaps occur at random that the viewer infers a fabrication error.

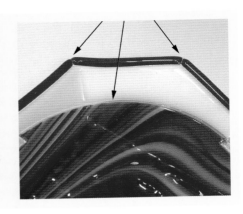

Dish Pan Hands

It's time to clean all my glass components. I prefer to wash my pieces in a plastic tub filled with water and a little dish soap right at my workbench. You could take your pieces to a sink if you have one handy but for me a plastic tub works just fine. The glass is not as susceptible to breakage in a plastic tub and I can continue to work at my bench without having to move my glass. I usually put the smaller pieces in to soak while I scrub the larger ones. I dry the pieces with a terry towel to make sure everything is squeaky clean.

Build Then Load

My glass cutting & fitting is done, my pre-fired components (wavy rods) are done, cleaning is done and I'm ready for final assembly. I prefer to complete my pre-fuse assembly directly on the kiln shelf at my workbench then secure everything with a little fusing glue. When the glue has set I carry the shelf with my project over to the kiln then lower it into the firing chamber. By the way, rigid fiberboard works great for this as well. You must have ample room inside your kiln to keep the shelf level as you lower it, without having to tilt it to fit past the thermocouple - if you're looking for a solution to this problem see ProTip: Keeping it On The Level, next page.

Pre-Fuse Assembly

I place a prepared kiln shelf on my bench then place a sheet of thin resist paper on the shelf. Now I position the base glass layer on the thin resist paper, this could be a single piece of glass (as mine is) or it could be a grouping of glass pieces or pre-fired components - whatever I need for my design. Then I stack the second layer pieces on top of the first and use a few drops of fusing glue to hold the positions. Finally I place my top-level design elements, for this project that would be my wavy rods, and use a little glue to secure those as well.

Survey Says

Give the glue sufficient time to set and use that time to survey the assembly and your design. Make sure the components are lined up the way you want them, use tweezers to reposition anything that is out of place. For this project I had a feeling that my design needed a little something extra around the border. I tried some yellow stringer but the color was too much. Then I tried 4 small black 'frit balls' offset in one corner and I liked how that looked. So I added the dots to all 4 corners.

ProTip: Keeping It 'On The Level'

With the shelf loaded you must keep it level while lowering it into the kiln. Unfortunately the thermocouple probe often gets in the way. If the probe in your kiln is movable you can pull it back, lower the shelf, then push the probe back in. But don't forget to push the probe back in or the temperature reading will be off and your firing will be ruined. The probe in my kiln is fixed and it sticks into the kiln 1 1/4" - 32 mm. My shelf was about 1/4" - 6 mm too big to slide past it. I solved the problem by using my ring saw to cut a semi-circular notch in the edge of my shelf to accommodate the probe.

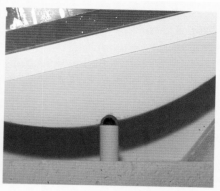

Load and Fire the Kiln

I always place three shelf supports on the kiln floor to create an air space below the shelf. The kiln floor is the coldest area inside the kiln and this space helps to balance the heat. I carefully lower my project assembly into the kiln and rest it on the shelf supports. Do a final check to make sure nothing shifted then close the lid. My kiln has a digital controller and I'll use that to set my firing schedule. Now I need to select a firing schedule that will successfully achieve the outcome I'm looking for.

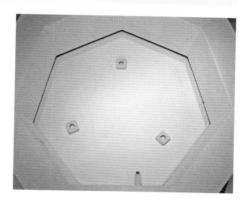

How Fused Do I Want It?

Of course I want my piece to be fused, but the 'final fuse point' can range from barely tacked all the way to full-flat smooth with many variations in between. If I cut and assembled two projects that were exact in every way at the pre-fire stage, then fired one of them to minimal-tack and the other one to full-fuse, they would look and feel completely different. The 'minimal-tack' piece would have square corners, sharper edges and raw-textured surface elements while the 'full-fuse' piece would have rounded-off corners, rounded edges and a smooth flat surface. Both styles would be considered 'fused' glass but from an artistic point of view the final fuse point is a fundamental choice (See pages 26 - 28 for fusing level images).

Is It Hot Enough For You?

So how do you know which fusing level will be the best one for your project? How do you know how hot to fire your kiln to get the result you're seeking? You'll get the answers by testing your kiln and controller, by creating a 'Fusing Level Sample Set'. It just so happens the next chapter is all about the 'Fusing Level Sample Set - so stay tuned. For now, I know I want to be able to use my bowl to serve a salad so it has to be completely smooth with no texture. The 'Sample' tile that I like is the FS5 - Full Fuse (it's on page 28) so I will set my digital controller to that firing schedule.

Hot Glass, Surface Tension, and Viscosity

This book is not a scientific journal (now that's an understatement) but the relationship between hot glass, surface tension, and viscosity is very important to understand, I promise to keep my explanation simple and to the point.

Surface Tension:

When glass is fired to full fuse temperature it will try to attain a thickness of 1/4" - 6 mm and this is the result of surface tension in the glass. The pull of surface tension is why a single layer of glass (1/8" - 3 mm) will shrink in size as it 'pulls up' attempting to become 1/4" - 6 mm thick. Conversely when 3 layers of glass (3/8" - 9 mm) are fused it will spread out and 'lower down' until the surface tension can hold it at 1/4" - 6 mm thick. Surface tension varies somewhat from one type of glass to another but the good news is that all glass manufactured for fusing has a surface tension that is close enough to be called the same.

Viscosity:

When glass is heated it will begin to flow. Viscosity is a measure of the 'fluidity' or 'runniness' of glass as it reaches optimum flow temperature. Glass with a low viscosity becomes runny more quickly over a narrower temperature range than a glass with a higher viscosity. There is some variance in the viscosity from one glass to the next, even within various glass manufactured for fusing. Viscosity variance explains why one glass seems to 'round off' or 'smooth out' at a certain temperature while another one doesn't. It also helps us to understand why the "soak period" at the final fuse temperature is an important consideration.

How to Stay Within the Ramp Speed Limit

Look at any firing chart on pages 26, 27 & 28 and you will notice that the middle column is the 'Ramp Rate' setting. The first line in that column is 'Primary Heat & Bubble Soak' and it says "See Ramp Rate Chart". So before we go any further we need to discuss ramp speeds.

Initial Heating Phase a.k.a. Ramp Rate

Every fusing artist has a personal philosophy when it comes to initial ramp up speed. Some like to play it safe and choose a slow and steady ramp speed for most firings plus an even slower speed when they have a 'high anxiety' project to fire. Other fusers, and I count myself in this category, prefer to take a calculated risk and choose the fastest ramp speed that (they hope) will safely and successfully fire that piece, in an effort to save time and electricity. (Note: I have been told that faster doesn't necessarily save on power, but it does save time and that's good enough for me). A safe ramp rate setting would be 300°F - 165°C per hour and a high-risk speed would be 900°F - 495°C per hour. The majority of firings will fall somewhere between these ramp speeds, however I will admit there are times when an even slower speed may be required.

Ramp speeds are listed as DPH - Degrees Per Hour. A speed of 500 F Degrees Per Hour - 275 C Degrees Per Hour indicates that the kiln will gain 500°F - 275°C over one hour. Simple math tells us that the kiln will reach 1000°F - 535°C in just under 2 hours (don't forget the kiln is starting at a room temperature of approximately 75°F - 25°C). On the other hand, a ramp speed of 300°F Per Hour - 165°C Per Hour will take more than three hours to reach 1000°F - 535°C (1000°F divided by 300 [535°C divided 165] equals 3.3 hours). So why not use 500°F PH - 275°C PH or even faster for everything? The reason is thermal shock. When glass is subjected to a rapid temperature change, either up or down, it will fracture. This reaction is called thermal shock.

Ramp Rate Charts

To prevent thermal shock we must calculate and control the rate of temperature change to keep it within the tolerance of the glass that is either heating or cooling.

Small pieces of glass are less prone to thermal shock and that's why jewelry projects can be ramped at 900°F - 495°C Per Hour with little problem. However when slumping a previously fused piece, say a 12" - 30 cm diameter, 2 layer thick blank into a ceramic bowl mold, the ramp speed must be reduced to 300°F Per Hour - 165°C Per Hour.

I've created a couple of charts to help me determine the best ramp rate for my projects. I measure the largest single piece of glass in my assembly (usually the base or the top cover). Then I select the corresponding size in the Ramp Rate Chart. The 'Diameter or Square' column in the chart gives a dimension for a circle or a square. If the largest piece is a rectangle or other odd shape I simply multiply the height times the width to get the area then use the 'Surface Area' column to confirm the ramp speed I can use safely.

Below are my Ramp Rate charts. I use the upper one for initial or first firings, when my project is made up using only single thick glass (1/8" - 3 mm). The lower chart is for subsequent firings where I am using pre-fused glass components that are double thick (1/4" - 6 mm) or whenever the firing uses a ceramic mold (a ceramic mold can thermal shock as well).

Note: These charts are only a rule of thumb, if I'm firing a high anxiety piece I will soften the risk by moving down the chart a line or 2 to a slower DPH.

Single Thick Glass - Initial Firings - Largest Glass Component

Relative Size Description	Diameter or Square (Inch)	Surface Area (Square Inch)	Degree Per Hour (Fahrenheit)	Diameter or Square (Centimeter)	Surface Area (Square Cm)	Degree Per Hour (Celsius)
Xtra-Small	Under 2.5	Under 7	900°F	Under 5	Under 25	495°C
Small	Up to 4	Up to 16	800°F	Up to 10	Up to 100	435°C
Small Plus	Up to 5	Up to 25	700°F	Up to 13	Up to 170	380°C
Med-Small	Up to 6 1/2	Up to 42	600°F	Up to 17	Up to 290	325°C
Medium	Up to 8	Up to 64	500°F	Up to 20	Up to 400	275°C
Med-Plus	Up to 10	Up to 100	400°F	Up to 25	Up to 625	220°C
Large	Up to 12	Up to 144	350°F	Up to 30	Up to 900	190°C
Xtra-Large	Over 12	Over 144	300°F	Over 30	Over 900	165°C

Double Thick Glass - Subsequent Firings - Largest Glass Component

Relative Size Description	Diameter or Square (Inch)	Surface Area (Square Inch)	Degree Per Hour (Fahrenheit)	Diameter or Square (Centimeter)	Surface Area (Square Cm)	Degree Per Hour (Celsius)
Xtra-Small	Under 2.5	Under 7	540°F	Under 5	Under 25	300°C
Small	Up to 4	Up to 16	480°F	Up to 10	Up to 100	260°C
Small Plus	Up to 5	Up to 25	420°F	Up to 13	Up to 170	230°C
Med-Small	Up to 6 1/2	Up to 42	380°F	Up to 17	Up to 290	205°C
Medium	Up to 8	Up to 64	360°F	Up to 20	Up to 400	195°C
Med-Plus	Up to 10	Up to 100	340°F	Up to 25	Up to 625	185°C
Large	Up to 12	Up to 144	320°F	Up to 30	Up to 900	175°C
Xtra-Large	Over 12	Over 144	300°F	Over 30	Over 900	165°C

Fusing Levels Sample Set - How fused do you want it?

From an artistic point of view the 'final fuse point (temperature + soak time)' is a fundamental consideration. The choice you make here will determine if your piece is completely fused with rounded corners and a smooth flat surface or if it will have minimally fire polished edges with well defined corners and an abundance of surface texture. There are numerous stages in between those fusing extremes but to keep things simple I've settled on six distinct levels and developed a firing schedule for each one. Then I designed and created a set of 6 tiles that use the same pattern and the same glass. In fact I created two sets of tiles - one using COE 96 and one using COE 90 glass. Then I placed one tile from each COE in my kiln and fired both of them at the same time using the same firing schedule. The only thing that changes from one schedule to the next is the 'final fuse point'. As you will see the results are really quite dramatic and I consult these sample tiles all the time when I'm trying to decide; "How fused do I want my piece to be?"

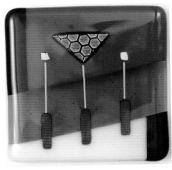

These tiles were cut from the same glass. The left one was fired to 1245°F - 675°C while the right was fired to 1425°F - 775°C

These 2 kilns may look the same but testing is still a good idea

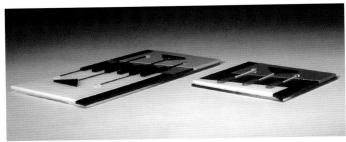

Both of these tiles were fired to an FS1 Elevated Tack schedule with a target temperature of 1245°F - 675°C and a hold-soak of 10 minutes. COE 96 is on the left and COE 90 is on the right

I Know, I Know - All Kilns Are Different

Every fusing instructor I've talked to and every fusing book I've read tells us that "All kilns are different and the appropriate temperature for any given result will vary." They recommend, "Test your kiln to find the best fuse-level temperatures". They are right of course; kilns do vary but the question is; "What's the best way to test a kiln?" My answer is "by creating a set of tiles that are precisely the same, then fire them using six progressively hotter firing schedules that will produce tiles from barley tacked to fully fused".

I have no doubt that an FS1 - 'Elevated Tack' firing (see FS1 on page 26) in your kiln will look somewhat different from the FS1 sample that I created in my kiln. But that comparison doesn't really matter. What does matter is for you to know exactly what a piece looks like when it has been fuse fired using the FS1 schedule in your kiln. Then when you're creating a new work all you have to do is pick the sample tile that matches the outcome you desire then set the kiln controller to fire according to that schedule and you're good to go.

ProTip: When You Want Even More Control

After you have created your Six Studio Samples you may want to refine the look of your piece to be 'a little more fused than an FS2 and little less fused than an FS3'. Simply adjust the final fuse point slightly to a mid point temperature or increase the soak time slightly or perhaps both - but be careful 'slightly' is a relative term. And if you do make this adjustment remember to make a notation in your project log (see page 17) so you can use it again if you liked the outcome - or remember to stay away from it if you didn't.

Temperature Differences Between COE Categories

As we've already discussed, the 2 most popular fusing glass categories are: COE 90 (Bullseye, Uroboros, Wasser & Wissmach) and COE 96 (Spectrum & Uroboros). You cannot mix glass from these 2 categories in the same project, however you can fire different projects from each COE in the same kiln load and that is exactly what I did for my sample panels. The prevailing view within the fusing community suggests that COE 96 glass tends to soften sooner and at a lower temperature than COE 90 glass. In theory that should mean that COE 90 glass requires a few degrees more heat and/or a few minutes longer soak to reach the same result (see Hot Glass, Surface Tension, and Viscosity on page 22). After close inspection of my finished sample panels I can see some tendency in that direction but from a practical standpoint the differences are negligible. The point is there is really no need to compare the outcome of one COE glass to the other, all that matters is to know exactly what a finished piece looks like when it has been fired using a given schedule. Then you can make an informed choice the next time you need to know; "How fused do you want it?"

Designs for the Studio Sample Tiles

Here are the designs that I created for my 2 layer sample tiles. I wanted to have a single piece clear base with a mix of opals & cathedrals on the 2nd layer (from white to black & in between). For the décor layer I wanted some geometric shapes, some large and small dichroic accents and some stringers. Feel free to create a design of your own or if you would like to use this design you can download the full-size pattern for free from the book's website, www.JoyOfFusing.com

Cut, Clean & Assemble

I selected my glass and cut all my panels at the same time to ensure all the glass was exactly the same (it's also faster to do it that way). I decided to make the larger panel using COE 96 and the smaller one using COE 90 but it really doesn't matter if you want to make all your samples using only the larger or the smaller design. What really does matter is you must keep the COE 90 glass separated from the COE 96! Follow the steps on pages 18 to 21 to assemble your first sample set on a prepared kiln shelf.

So Let's Fire the Sample Panels

The largest single piece in my sample tile is 4" x 8" - 10 cm x 20 cm. That's an area of 32 Square Inches - area of 200 SqCm. The Ramp Rate Chart on page 23 (Single Thick - Initial Firing) tells me to use the Med-Small ramp up of 600°F Per Hour - 360°C Per Hour. I will fire one set of panels following each of the 6 firing schedules shown on the next 3 pages. The only difference in these firing schedules is the Final Target Temperature - with each one increasing from 40°F to 55°F - 20°C to 30°C for each new firing (more on that in the Conclusion section on page 29).

When You're Ready - Just Do It

Place the assembled sample panels in the kiln, program the digital controller for FS1 (Fusing Schedule 1), close the lid and hit the switch.

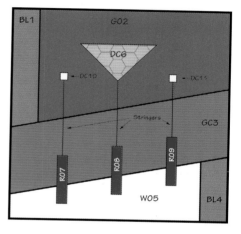

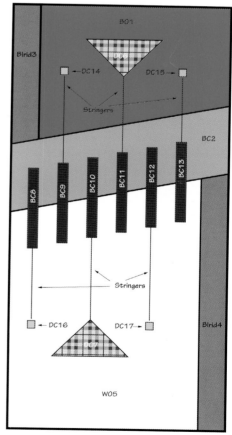

FS1 - Elevated Tack

COE 96 Glass

All glass components are firmly stuck together and the surface is fire polished but the edges are only slightly blunted. The stringers, the dichroic triangles and other elements are elevated and retain an undistorted shape that produces a sculptural appearance.

The edges are crisp and the décor pieces are fully elevated

COE 90 Glass

FS1 - Elevated Tack Schedule

Segment Description	Segment Number	Ramp Rate Degree Per Hour	Final Target Temperature	Hold-Soak Minutes
Primary Heat & Bubble Soak	1	See Ramp Rate Chart	1150 °F - 635 °C	30
Intention Heat & Target Soak	2	300 °F - 165 °C	1245 °F - 675 °C	10
Rapid Drop to Anneal Soak	3	AFAP Full or 9999	950 °F - 510 °C	45
Slow Descent Anneal Cool	4	125 °F - 67 °C	700 °F - 370 °C	0
Power-off Cool to Room Temp	5	0000 Kiln Off	75 °F - 25 °C Room Temp	Do Not Open Kiln

FS2 - Dimensional Tack

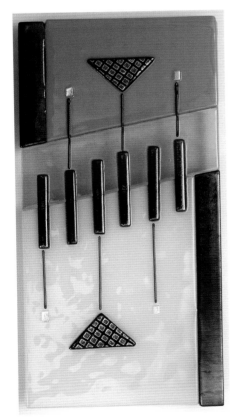

COE 96 Glass

The outside edges are rounding slightly and the surface is fully fire polished. The stringers are beginning to melt into the surface glass but are still raised with a pronounced texture. The space between adjoining pieces on the 2nd layer have opened up slightly to form an attractive channel.

Edges are blunting but the décor texture is still very strong

COE 90 Glass

FS2 - Dimensional Tack Schedule

Segment Description	Segment Number	Ramp Rate Degree Per Hour	Final Target Temperature	Hold-Soak Minutes
Primary Heat & Bubble Soak	1	See Ramp Rate Chart	1150 °F - 635 °C	30
Intention Heat & Target Soak	2	300 °F - 165 °C	1290 °F - 700 °C	10
Rapid Drop to Anneal Soak	3	AFAP Full or 9999	950 °F - 510 °C	45
Slow Descent Anneal Cool	4	125 °F - 67 °C	700 °F - 370 °C	0
Power-off Cool to Room Temp	5	0000 Kiln Off	75 °F - 25 °C Room Temp	Do Not Open Kiln

The surface decoration layer retains a pronounced raised texture that is about 50% of the original glass thickness. The edges and corners are rounding off and the spaces are beginning to fill in. Perfect level for any piece where the surface texture is important to the design.

The décor layer glass is about 50% of its original thickness

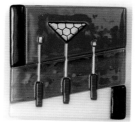

COE 90 Glass

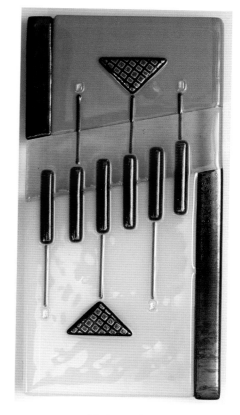

FS3 - Texture Fuse Schedule				
Segment Description	Segment Number	Ramp Rate Degree Per Hour	Final Target Temperature	Hold-Soak Minutes
Primary Heat & Bubble Soak	1	See Ramp Rate Chart	1150 °F - 635 °C	30
Intention Heat & Target Soak	2	300 °F - 165 °C	1330 °F - 720 °C	10
Rapid Drop to Anneal Soak	3	AFAP Full or 9999	950 °F - 510 °C	45
Slow Descent Anneal Cool	4	125 °F - 67 °C	700 °F - 370 °C	0
Power-off Cool to Room Temp	5	0000 Kiln Off	75 °F - 25 °C Room Temp	Do Not Open Kiln

COE 96 Glass

This tile is about 80% of the way to a full-fuse. The edges and corners are almost fully rounded off but the top surface still has a lot of texture. This is a very popular fusing level because the viewer can see and feel the texture from the décor pieces, while presenting a full fused effect.

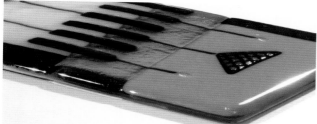

Edges have rounded but there is still lots of surface texture

COE 90 Glass

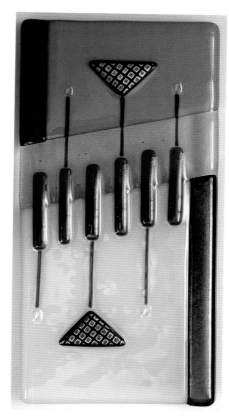

FS4 - Contour Fuse Schedule				
Segment Description	Segment Number	Ramp Rate Degree Per Hour	Final Target Temperature	Hold-Soak Minutes
Primary Heat & Bubble Soak	1	See Ramp Rate Chart	1150 °F - 635 °C	30
Intention Heat & Target Soak	2	300 °F - 165 °C	1370 °F - 745 °C	10
Rapid Drop to Anneal Soak	3	AFAP Full or 9999	950 °F - 510 °C	45
Slow Descent Anneal Cool	4	125 °F - 67 °C	700 °F - 370 °C	0
Power-off Cool to Room Temp	5	0000 Kiln Off	75 °F - 25 °C Room Temp	Do Not Open Kiln

COE 96 Glass

FS5 - Full Fuse

COE 96 Glass

The surface of this tile is 97% flat - only the dichroic-on-black triangles are ever so slightly raised. The corners and edges are completely rounded off and the surface is slick and shiny. This panel was 2 full layers plus design layer so the edges on the square shape remain relatively straight.

Tile is 97% flat, the dichroic-on-black is raised only slightly

COE 90 Glass

FS5 - Full Fuse Schedule				
Segment Description	Segment Number	Ramp Rate Degree Per Hour	Final Target Temperature	Hold-Soak Minutes
Primary Heat & Bubble Soak	1	See Ramp Rate Chart	1150 °F - 635 °C	30
Intention Heat & Target Soak	2	300 °F - 165 °C	1425 °F - 775 °C	10
Rapid Drop to Anneal Soak	3	AFAP Full or 9999	950 °F - 510 °C	45
Slow Descent Anneal Cool	4	125 °F- 67 °C	700 °F - 370 °C	0
Power-off Cool to Room Temp	5	0000 Kiln Off	75 °F - 25 °C Room Temp	Do Not Open Kiln

FS6 - Deep Fuse

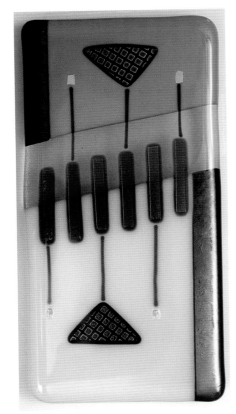

COE 96 Glass

The surface of this tile is 100% flat. The only difference between this firing and the previous FS5 - Full Fuse firing is the dichroic-on-black triangles are now completely flat. The thickness is the same, there is a slight bump on the left edge but the overall effect is more or less the same.

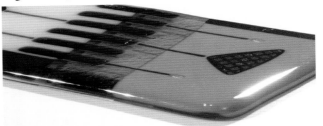

Tile is 100% flat with a smooth surface & rounded edges

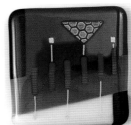

COE 90 Glass

FS6 - Deep Fuse Schedule				
Segment Description	Segment Number	Ramp Rate Degree Per Hour	Final Target Temperature	Hold-Soak Minutes
Primary Heat & Bubble Soak	1	See Ramp Rate Chart	1150 °F - 635 °C	30
Intention Heat & Target Soak	2	300 °F - 165 °C	1470 °F - 800 °C	10
Rapid Drop to Anneal Soak	3	AFAP Full or 9999	950 °F - 510 °C	45
Slow Descent Anneal Cool	4	125 °F- 67 °C	700 °F - 370 °C	0
Power-off Cool to Room Temp	5	0000 Kiln Off	75 °F - 25 °C Room Temp	Do Not Open Kiln

Conclusion - What Did We Learn?

For me the most surprising result is the rather subtle difference between any two adjacent tiles in the series. There is an observable difference but the divergence is not as much as you might think. However the difference between the 1st, the 3rd and the 5th tile is quite dramatic. The reason I recommend 6 final fuse points is to make an allowance for the diversity between kilns and to take the variation between glass colors, glass types and glass manufacturing processes into account.

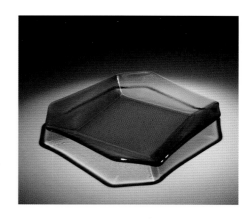

What if Your Elevated Tack Doesn't Look Like Ours?

It would be nice if everything in life were entirely predictable (actually that would be a little boring). The fact is pyrometers are calibrated differently and different kilns heat and cool differently. The perfect fuse point for an Elevated Tack in my kiln is 1245°F - 675°C with a 10 minute soak and from my experience there is a good chance that schedule will be very close for your kiln as well. So unless you know differently the FS1 firing schedule on page 26 is a great place to start but you must analyze the outcome to make sure it matches the image and description. If your's doesn't it's important to make an adjustment and then try another firing until you find the perfect fuse point for an Elevated Tack in your kiln. Then use that fuse point for your starting FS1 and adjust the other schedules using the same temperature increments that I used.

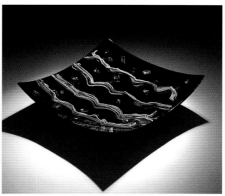

Annealing - The Final Frontier

The purpose of annealing is to relieve the internal stress in the glass created during the normal heating & cooling cycle of the kiln forming process. Anytime glass has been heated to the point of softening it must be rebalanced (de-stressed) during cool down by soaking at a constant temperature (around 950°F - 510°C) for a certain period of time (determined by volume) then cooled slowly until it has passed below the strain point (about 750°F - 400°C).

The 1st stage of annealing is the soak at 950°F - 510°C, this enables the fused glass piece, the kiln shelf, and the mold (if one is present) to equalize in temperature. The glass piece has just been subjected to traumatic heating to the point of melting then the temperature is reduced (sometimes rapidly) until the glass begins to solidify. The topside of the glass will be several degrees cooler than the bottom side that is in contact with the kiln shelf (or mold). The purpose of the anneal soak is to give the glass and its environment a chance to achieve temperature balance and allow it to de-stress from the fusing experience.

The 2nd stage of annealing is a controlled cooling that enables the now equalized temperature to remain 'in balance' until the glass has passed through the strain point temperature of 750°F - 400°C. This is achieved using a cool down ramp rate of 125°F - 67°C per hour from the soak temperature to 700°F - 370°C. But the glass is not out of the woods yet. If the kiln is opened, even for a few seconds, thermal shock is very likely. The kiln must remain closed and allowed to cool slowly at its natural rate until it is 100°F - 38°C.

It is difficult to find a consensus for a harmonized anneal soak temperature, hold time period and cool down rate. This is due to the many variables involved in the manufacture and structure of the glass itself, the type and size of the fused piece, the processes that the glass was subject to during kiln forming, plus other factors. The annealing procedure that is integrated into the firing schedules of this book was developed and successfully used for every small to medium-sized project that is in this book. If you intend to move beyond of this type and size of fusing project you may need to revisit and adjust these annealing numbers.

A Studio Sample Set - It's Worth the Effort

This Fusing Level Sample Set is a valuable resource for every fusing artist's studio. They can be a lot of fun to make (if you choose the right design) but more importantly you will learn so much about your kiln and the fusing process.

Glass Art Skills 101

The sample set is a spectacular art piece in and of itself, especially when the tiles are mounted for display on the wall of your studio. The photos on this page illustrate 2 distinctive ways to mount a Fusing Level Sample Set to combine striking good-looks with practical functionality. I refer to my samples regularly, particularly when I need to make a decision on the fuse level for a new project.

Kiln Function Skills 102

Making these 6 tiles is a painless way to conduct a definitive test of your kiln. You'll gain in depth knowledge about how your kiln works and become skilled at setting and changing the firing schedules in the digital controller. You'll figure out the best way to load your kiln either by pre-building on the shelf then loading (my favorite way) or by doing the pre-fuse assembly inside the kiln. You'll see first hand what happens to the glass at specific final fuse points. Note: A 'final fuse point' is the combination of final temperature plus soak time.

Fabrication Skills 103

The key fabrication objective here is to create six tiles that are exactly the same size, use the same glass and have the same decoration details. This is a challenge in itself and you will undoubtedly discover or invent some fabrication methods to help you achieve the uniform design that you seek. This new-found expertise will come in handy the next time you are working through the pre-fuse assembly of a future glass creation.

This is my COE 90 sample set mounted in a 12" x 24" - 30 x 60 cm picture frame that I purchased inexpensively at a department store. The Fusing Level tiles were secured to the picture frame glass using clear silicone. The tile in lower left is an FS1 - Elevated Tack sample that I used to balance my display.

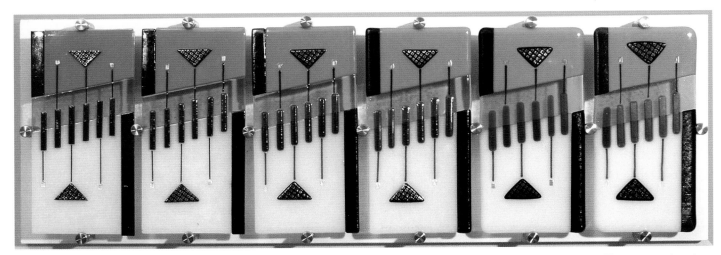

This is my System 96 Fusing Level sample set. The tiles are secured to a white board using stainless steel 'stand-off' mounting brackets that hold the tiles 1" - 25 mm away from the board. It is an elegant and very professional presentation for my studio wall.

Joy of Fusing - Fusing Basics, Molds & More

Testing... Testing... Your Glass on Fire

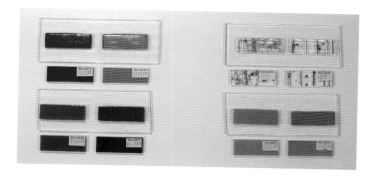

Glass fusing is all about the variables. Knowledge and experience gives us the ability to anticipate the surprises and deal with the differences. Glass color and texture is one variable that can have a dramatic affect on the outcome of our work.

Many colors will shift and change in subtle ways but some colors shift dramatically. The footed vase shown here is a good example. I alternated blue opal and black strips for this drop mold project. As you can see, when the final piece came out of the kiln my blue stripes had changed to more of a purple.

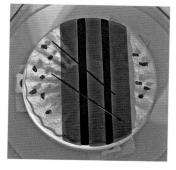
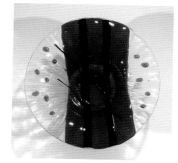

Glass manufacturers know that some of their colors change during fuse firing and sometimes you will find a sticker warning you that this color will shift during firing. The sticker on this orange OpalArt by Spectrum Glass says 'Darkens when Fired. I used that glass for the center circle in this bowl and as you can see it darkened from orange to burgundy.

More often than not a change in color is caused by an adjacent color in your design stack. For example a wispy glass fired over clear will look entirely different than if it were fired over white opal. Of course if a wispy or cathedral color were fired over a darker blue, red or black the color influence would be heightened even more.

The wispy glass in the 4th photo was slumped fired into a mold without being combined with any other glass. Even so the color change was quite dramatic.

In addition there are colors that are called 'reactive' that create an 'interface' color when they are melted against certain other colors. This new interface color is often a narrow outline or border that can range from a deep red, to earth tones, to black. Check with your favorite glass manufacturer for their reactive color list to find some new possibilities to explore.

The only way to know for sure what color changes may happen is to create a set of test fired samples. The photo at the top of this page are test fired samples on a clear base glass. The sample firing shown at right (still in the kiln) is an example of a test set I made using clear dichroic chips. After firing they were barely visible on the clear glass base but can be seen easily on the black base. The dichroic on black samples formed a black border that outlined the dichroic. All good information that I can use in future creations.

Mold Forming Techniques

Mold forming is an important process to master because the vast majority of fused projects are shaped, one way or another, into a 3-dimensional object. The first part of the fusing process usually involves creating a flat glass design that is fuse-fired to form a 'blank'. Then this flat 'blank' is placed on a mold for an additional firing, to be slumped or draped into a 3D object.

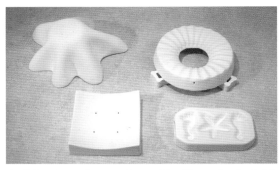

A Selection of ceramic molds (from back left): drape - deep bowl; drop ring - shallow vase; slump - shallow 'sushi' plate; casting - seahorse & starfish

Brush painting a mold with liquid primer

Spray painting a mold with liquid primer using a pump up garden sprayer

Slump, Drape or Cast Forming

There are 3 basic ways to mold form glass - slumping, draping and casting. Slumping is when the central area of the glass sinks into the cavity of a mold (see page 34). Draping is when the outer perimeter of the glass bends over the outside a mold (see page 35). Casting has numerous modes, but the most basic definition (and the one covered in this book) is to fill the design pocket of a casting mold with glass shards or frit then heat it until the glass has melted and fully-shaped into the mold cavity (see pages 68 and 70). Dropping is a variation of slumping where a ring mold is elevated off the kiln shelf then a glass blank is heated until it slumps into the ring mold and allowed to continue to drop through the central hole until it reaches the kiln shelf directly below (see page 64).

Please Release Me

Before you can use any mold to form glass it must be properly coated with a glass release or resist (see page 14 & 15). Most fusers, including myself, use shelf primer on ceramic molds however a concentrated variety of boron nitride spray (similar to spray paint in a can) is available that works very well on ceramic molds. For stainless steel molds I prefer the boron nitride spray because it coats evenly, sticks to the stainless steel extremely well and holds up for multiple firings.

I prefer to apply the primer to my molds and shelves using a pump-up atomizer/sprayer (from a garden supply store). The sprayer works best with a mix of 1 part powder with 6 parts water, which is much thinner than the mix used for brushing (usually 1 to 4). I spray the molds with 4 or 5 very light coats, allowing 5 minutes between coats to get a smooth cover every time. I like to heat dry my molds in a 500°F - 260°C kiln for 20 minutes. Heat drying seems to stabilize the primer providing a few extra firings before it needs to be stripped and recoated.

Developing a Template from a Mold

It is important to have a template that accurately fits the mold before you cut the base glass or fuse a glass blank. Sometimes making a template is as easy as measuring the diameter, the square or the rectangle size of the mold then reduce that dimension by 1/2" - 1 cm to ensure the blank is inside the top perimeter of the mold. For example a circular plate mold with a top diameter of 12 1/2" - 30 cm can handle a fused blank of 12" - 29 cm maximum. An 8" - 20 cm square mold would need a square blank of 7 1/2" - 19 cm maximum.

Sometimes the easiest way to create the template is to turn the mold upside down then trace the outline on paper, then redraw the outline making a 1/4" - 5 mm allowance all around. Be forewarned - whenever I try to push the size of a blank to match the top perimeter of the mold (without making an allowance) I invariably get a hangover somewhere along the edge (4th photo). If the hangover is really severe, the glass can 'trap' the mold as it cools. When this happens either the glass will break under the stress or you will not be able to remove the glass from the mold.

Single Layer Forming

When I get a new mold I like to create a cardboard template then cut and shape-fire a single piece of glass using that template, just to see how it looks. This way I'll know what to expect when I'm creating a designed piece for that mold. I'll know where to put the color or texture to get the most out of the shape. Sometimes I will create an odd shaped cardboard template, for example an oval template for a round or square shaped mold, then cut and shape-fire a single piece of clear glass to see how that looks. You'll be amazed at how many interesting shapes and uses you can get from one mold (see photo below right).

Mold Forming Schedule

This all-purpose schedule will cover most of the slumping or draping that you will do. The variable in the schedule is the 'Primary Heat' - 'Ramp Rate'. Use the ramp rate chart on page 23 to select the Degree Per Hour according to the size of your blank. The 'Target Soak' - time has been set for 10 minutes and that should be ideal for the majority of slump and drape firings. You will encounter projects that would benefit from a longer 'Target Soak' time. Some of the possible considerations are: when slumping into a very deep mold, one that has a steep side angle, sharp corner angles or narrow ridges to name only a few. In addition the viscosity and thickness of the glass will have an effect on the outcome.

Measuring a square mold for flat size

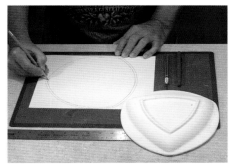
Creating a template to fit a slump mold

Test fire a single piece to see how it looks

A mold edge hangover, blank was too big

MF1 - Mold Forming Schedule				
Segment Description	Segment Number	Ramp Rate Degree Per Hour	Final Target Temperature	Hold-Soak Minutes
Primary Heat & Balance Soak	1	See Ramp Rate Chart	1000°F - 540°C	10
Intention Heat & Target Soak	2	300°F - 165°C	1260°F - 682°C	10
Rapid Drop to Anneal Soak	3	AFAP Full or 9999	950°F - 510°C	45
Slow Descent Anneal Cool	4	125°F - 67°C	700°F - 370°C	0
Power-off Cool to Room Temp	5	0000 Kiln Off	75°F - 25°C Room Temp	Do Not Open Kiln

A rectangle on a square mold? - it works!

Project 1 Fluted Serving Platter

Project at a Glance

Finished Project Size:
- 10 1/2" dia x 1" - 27 x 2.5 cm

Mold: Ceramic
- 12 1/2" - 32 cm diameter plate style with 24 accordion flutes

Kiln Firings: 1 Only
- MF1 - Mold Forming

Glass & Components:
- Blown Antique glass, single layer (non-fusing glass)

10 1/2" - 27 cm
Diameter

I wanted to create an elegant serving platter with this beautiful hand blown streaky glass. I have a plate mold with deep 'accordion pleats' that should enhance the streaks in the glass.

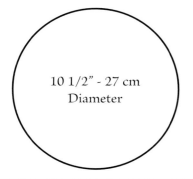

Measure to determine the blank size

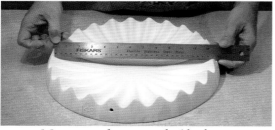

Clean blank is centered on the slump mold

Draped plate still on mold after cool down

This mold can handle a 12" - 30.5 cm diameter disk but I wanted a smaller plate so I used my swing arm circle cutter to score a 10 1/2" - 27 cm disk. A slump firing is not hot enough to fully round the edge so I squared the edge with a medium abrasive grinding bit then changed to a extra-fine 'Fusing' bit and lifted the disk about 30° to put a slight bevel on both sides.

I centered the disk on the mold in the kiln and set the kiln controller to the **MF1 - Mold Forming**. I used the 'Double Thick Glass' Ramp Rate chart to set 320°F - 175°C ramp per hour and I increased the target soak time to 40 minutes to give this thicker 'non-fusible' glass a chance to settle more into the deep pleats.

The platter turned out beautifully. The surface and edge are glossy with no devitrification. The glass did not fully slump to the bottom of the deep pleats (even with a longer soak) but I actually prefer the rounder flutes as opposed to the more angular pleats.

MF1 - Mold Forming Schedule				
Segment Description	Segment Number	Ramp Rate Degree Per Hour	Final Target Temperature	Hold-Soak Minutes
Primary Heat & Balance Soak	1	320°F - 175°C	1000°F - 540°C	10
Intention Heat & Target Soak	2	300°F - 165°C	1260°F - 682°C	40
Rapid Drop to Anneal Soak	3	AFAP Full or 9999	950°F - 510°C	45
Slow Descent Anneal Cool	4	125°F - 67°C	700°F - 370°C	0
Power-off Cool to Room Temp	5	0000 Kiln Off	75°F - 25°C Room Temp	Do Not Open Kiln

Drapery Folds Bowl
Project 2

Project at a Glance

Finished Project Size:
• 10" diameter x 3 1/2" - 25 x 9 cm

Mold: Ceramic
• 12" dia (at widest point) x 4" high - 30 cm x 10 cm high, bowl style with 6 drapery flutes

Kiln Firings: 1 Only
• MF1 - Mold Forming

Glass & Components:
• Blown Antique glass, single layer (non-fusing glass)

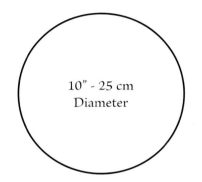

10" - 25 cm
Diameter

The pre-fire procedure for this bowl is easy. Cut a 10" - 25 cm diameter circle, grind the edge to round it off slightly then vigorously clean both sides (fingerprints are not allowed).

The drape mold that I'm using produces a shape that is similar to draping over a floral former (see photo). Working with a floral former can be exciting. You get a different shape every time but you must watch as it begins to drape, then flash cool to freeze the shape. On the other hand using a fixed-shape drape mold like this one allows me to set my kiln to automatically run the mold forming schedule and I know exactly what the shape will be.

My kiln is 6 1/2" - 15 cm from floor to lid and this mold is 4" - 10 cm high. I placed the shelf directly on the floor of the kiln to create as much space as possible between the glass and the hot elements in the lid. I put the mold on the shelf, centered the glass then set the controller to the **MF1 - Mold Forming** schedule with a ramp rate of 300°F - 165°C to compensate for the glass being so close to the heating elements and a target soak time of 30 minutes to enable it to drop more deeply into the drapery folds.

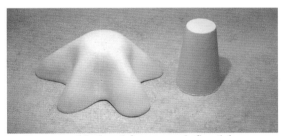
Drape molds, bowl former and floral former

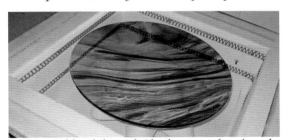
Drape mold in kiln with blank centered and ready

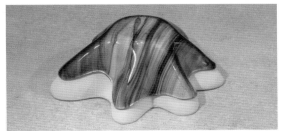
Draped bowl still on mold after cooling

MF1 - Mold Forming Schedule

Segment Description	Segment Number	Ramp Rate Degree Per Hour	Final Target Temperature	Hold-Soak Minutes
Primary Heat & Balance Soak	1	300°F - 165°C	1000°F - 540°C	10
Intention Heat & Target Soak	2	300°F - 165°C	1260°F - 682°C	30
Rapid Drop to Anneal Soak	3	AFAP Full or 9999	950°F - 510°C	45
Slow Descent Anneal Cool	4	125°F - 67°C	700°F - 370°C	0
Power-off Cool to Room Temp	5	0000 Kiln Off	75°F - 25°C Room Temp	Do Not Open Kiln

Bars & Stripes Tray

Project at a Glance

Finished Project Size:
- 11 1/2" x 7 1/2" x 3/4"
  - 29 x 19 x 2 cm

Mold: Stainless Steel
- 12 1/2" x 8 1/2" - 32 x 22 cm, oval

Kiln Firings: 2 Total
- FS4 - Contour Fuse
- MF1 - Mold Forming

Glass & Components:
- Base Layer: Clear with pink fractures & black streamers
- Design Layer: Irid white opal, spaghetti stringers assorted colors

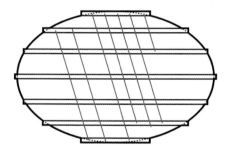

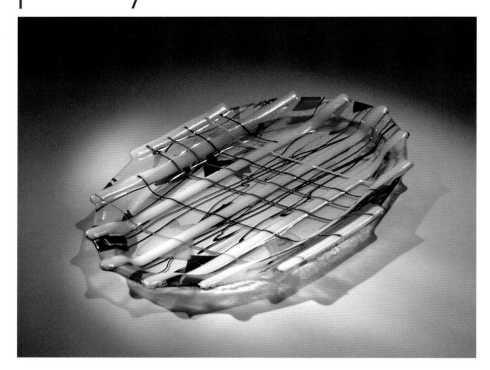

The clear fracture and streamer glass has a lot going on already and the white opal strips bring order to the design while the colorful spaghetti stringers add a layer of playfulness.

Trace template oval using a sharpie then cut the glass

I traced the stainless steel mold and then created an oval template that was 1/4" - 6 mm smaller. The project has only the fracture and streamer base layer and a decor layer. I started by cutting the oval base layer. I set up my portable jig system to cut enough 1/4" - 6 mm iridized white opal strips for the bars, plus one additional strip cut from the clear fusible glass.

My major design objective was to allow the narrow white strips to extend beyond the oval border of the base glass. To accomplish this correctly I needed to have support tabs cut from the clear base glass that could be placed under the white opal extensions.

Using a portable jig system to cut the narrow white bars

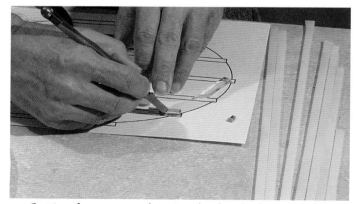

Cutting the support tabs using the clear background glass

Bars & Stripes Tray

I placed the 1/4" - 6 mm clear strip (that I had cut earlier) on my layout drawing and cut these tiny but very important support tabs (see photo previous page bottom right). Then I trimmed my white opal strips to length according to the layout drawing.

To begin the assembly I placed a sheet of thin resist paper on the kiln shelf then positioned the oval clear in the middle and secured the oval to the sheet with a little glue. Next I positioned the 7 white strips across the oval then slipped the clear support tabs under the ends (see photo at right) and used some glue to keep these tabs in place. The final assembly step was to trim and place 6 colorful spaghetti stringers on a diagonal across the white bars. By the way, the black marker line on the base oval is there to assist in the layout - it will burn off completely and will not stain the glass.

I loaded the assembly into my kiln and fired it using the **FS4 - Contour Fuse** schedule.

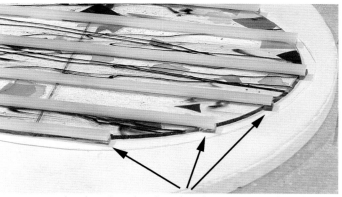

Support tabs placed under the white bars & secured with glue

FS4 - Contour Fuse Schedule

Segment Description	Segment Number	Ramp Rate Degree Per Hour	Final Target Temperature	Hold-Soak Minutes
Primary Heat & Bubble Soak	1	400°F - 220°C	1150°F - 635°C	30
Intention Heat & Target Soak	2	300°F - 165°C	1370°F - 745°C	10
Rapid Drop to Anneal Soak	3	AFAP Full or 9999	950°F - 510°C	45
Slow Descent Anneal Cool	4	125°F - 67°C	700°F - 370°C	0
Power-off Cool to Room Temp	5	0000 Kiln Off	75°F - 25°C Room Temp	Do Not Open Kiln

Placing the spaghetti stringers across the top of the white bars

After my fused blank had cooled I placed it on my stainless steel tray mold (that had been sprayed with boron nitride). Then set my controller to the following **MF1 - Mold Forming** schedule - using an initial ramp rate of 340°F - 185°C (taken from the Ramp Rate Chart on page 23). Then turned the kiln on.

MF1 - Mold Forming Schedule

Segment Description	Segment Number	Ramp Rate Degree Per Hour	Final Target Temperature	Hold-Soak Minutes
Primary Heat & Balance Soak	1	340°F - 185°C	1000°F - 540°C	10
Intention Heat & Target Soak	2	300°F - 165°C	1260°F - 682°C	10
Rapid Drop to Anneal Soak	3	AFAP Full or 9999	950°F - 510°C	45
Slow Descent Anneal Cool	4	125°F - 67°C	700°F - 370°C	0
Power-off Cool to Room Temp	5	0000 Kiln Off	75°F - 25°C Room Temp	Do Not Open Kiln

First review after firing to an FS4 - Contour Fuse - looks good!

Finished piece still on the mold in the kiln after the slump firing

Tutorial - Strip Fabrication

Narrow glass strips are so versatile that I keep a stash of them in my studio at all times. The projects in this chapter require narrow strips, from 1/4" to 3/8" - 7 to 10 mm wide, while other projects have borders made from wider strips. In fact, more than half of the projects in this book have components that require straight-line cuts, such as, borders, rectangles, squares, triangles, etc. If you're new to glass cutting you may be thinking, "So what's the big deal?" But if you've been cutting glass for a while you know how difficult it can be to make a quality score using a straight edge.

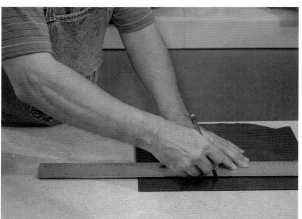

Pulling the cutter to follow a straight edge ruler

Pushing the cutter to follow the edge of an L-square

The Straight Scoop on Straight-Line Cuts

The secret to scoring along a straight edge is to keep your wrist and elbow steady as you move the cutter. This is more difficult than it sounds. We have a tendency to swing our elbow out and twist our wrist as we push or pull the cutter along a straight edge and this causes the cutter head to wander. Most professional glasscutters have a pivoting head - to compensate for this natural twisting and that would be great if we would simply let it happen, unfortunately most of us unconsciously over-compensate by turning the glasscutter into the ruler - to make sure it doesn't stray. We don't even realize that we are doing this but I have found that almost everyone does. When this happens the glasscutter is no longer rolling smoothly on-center, instead it is scraping along the ruler at an angle, creating a scratch rather than a quality score - and that spells disaster.

When I'm scoring with a straight edge I like to pull my glasscutter from the far edge of the glass towards me (see middle photo). Many crafters prefer to push their glasscutter, as I'm doing in the lower photo. Either method is fine, what really matters is to keep the cutter wheel running parallel to the straight edge. Practice making straight edge scores using an L-square (aka: glass square) and some scrap clear glass. It will take 30 or 40 attempts until you really get the hang of it - but since so many fusing projects require a straight edge score, the effort to master this technique is worth it.

ProTip: No-Brainer Straight Edge Scoring

We have some very clever inventors in our glass industry and a new cutter assist tool called a 'Sure-Score' has come to my attention. This device is a 4" x 19" - 10 x 50 cm clear Plexiglas board with 2 slots cut down the center (it also has inch and centimeter marks). You align one of the slots in the 'Sure-Score' with the line you intend to cut, place the cutter head into the slot then push or pull your cutter to score along the line. The slot in the 'Sure-Score' board restrains the cutter head, holding it precisely parallel to the score line - no matter what kind of twisting movement your hand makes. This ingenious device really does work and it instantly solves any straight line scoring troubles a crafter may have, without having to learn anything new.

Scoring Devices and Pattern Guide Systems

Every glass studio needs an L-square and a 36" - 1 meter straight edge ruler. Whenever I need to cut a large sheet in half, I prefer to use my large 36" - 1 meter L-square, but a 36" - 1 meter ruler works too. I'll use my smaller 13" - 33 cm L-square when I'm dividing a sheet of glass into smaller working components, or when a project needs only one rectangle, a square, or perhaps a few border strips.

Whenever I need larger quantity of border strips, squares or any other geometric shape, I use my portable jig system. There are several brands of strip cutting devices and systems available to help you automate strip cutting. Don't forget strips aren't always long and narrow. Sometimes I will cut an inch strip, then turn it 90° and continue to cut one inch pieces to create a series of squares (see Project 11 on page 56) and there are so many other applications. A portable jig system is a real timesaver and instantly increases cutting accuracy, lifting your art to the next level. Be sure to ask your local art glass retailer for a jig system demonstration and recommendation (see ProTip: Dancing the Jig on page 11).

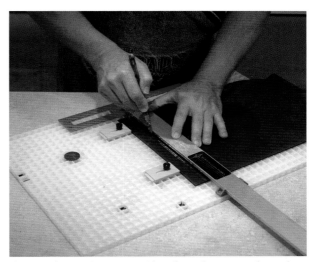

Using the Morton Portable Glass Shop to make strips

Stash On Hand

I always have an assortment of glass strips pre-cut and ready to use. I have a stash of clear plus light to medium colors of cathedral glass, all cut into narrow strips from 1/4" to 3/8" - 7 to 10 mm wide. I keep these strips in plastic tubs, one for clear and one for the mixed colors. Whenever my stash is getting low I purchase either a half or quarter sheet and cut the entire sheet into narrow strips. Then whenever I want to make something quick or that doesn't require a lot of pre-planning, I choose this strip fabrication technique to have a little fun while making a spectacular art piece.

Pre-cut strips in storage bins ready for the next strip fabrication project. The bin on the left has a full sheet-worth of smooth clear while the bin on the right has an assortment of 6 light to medium cathedral colors.

Lattice Weave Platter

Project at a Glance

Finished Project Size:
- 7" x 12" x 3/4" - 18 x 30 x 2 cm

Mold: Ceramic
- 7 1/2" x 12 1/2" - 19 x 30.5 cm rectangle, sushi style

Kiln Firings: 2 Total
- FS4 - Contour Fuse
- MF1 - Mold Forming

Glass & Components:
- Base & 2nd Layer: clear & assorted light to medium cathedral colors

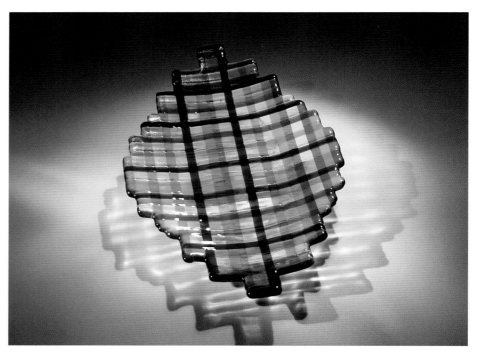

The unique stair step perimeter of this platter was created in a very simple way. The entire piece is made using narrow strips of clear and light to medium colors of cathedral glass.

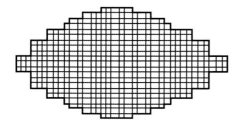

Measure to determine the blank size

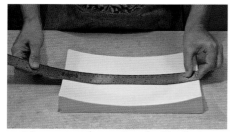

Begin the assembly with the center strips

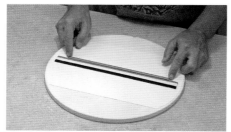

Continue until the width is reached

I measured the mold and found it can handle a 12" x 7" - 30 x 18 cm shape. I cut the central strips to the full length but I'll have to use a mixture of 1/4" & 3/8" - 7 & 10 mm wide strips to get the overall width as close as possible. I'm not aiming for precision I'm more concerned with a pleasing color pattern. I like to use a ratio of 1/3 clear to 2/3 cathedral colors, I have tried using more color but the panel becomes too dark.

The glass strips need to be cleaned before they are placed so I gather an assortment of colored and clear strips and put them in my washtub to soak for a few minutes then I take them out and pat them dry on a terry towel. Then I'll use my mosaic nippers to custom cut each strip to length and further cleaning will not be necessary.

I placed a sheet of thin resist paper on the kiln shelf then arranged the bottom layer of lattice strips in an rough oval pattern like this:

- 3 strips 12" - 30 cm long in the center
- 6 strips 10" - 25 cm long, 3 pcs on either side
- 4 strips 8" - 20 cm long, 2 pcs either side
- 2 strips 6" - 15 cm long, 1 pc either side
- 2 strips 5" - 13 cm long, 1 pc either side
- 2 strips 4" - 10 cm long, 1 pc either side
- 2 strips 2" - 5 cm long, 1 pc either side

This gave me the smooth stair-step oval that I wanted and it was very close to my target of 7" - 18 cm wide.

Lattice Weave Platter

Lay the 2nd layer of strips at 90° across the base oval. Starting at the center I measure and custom cut each strip to fit across the space. When I reach one of the stair step shoulders I select a strip width that will fit the corner properly. I work my way out to the ends, custom fitting each piece to the space as needed.

I want to maintain the stair step corners as sharp as possible but I also want the edges to be rounded off a little. I checked my studio sample tiles and picked the **FS4 - Contour Fuse** schedule. If you prefer to have a flat-smooth top surface you could choose an FS5 Full Fuse schedule (pg 28) however a full fuse will severely round off the stair-step corners. For me, keeping those corners as square as possible is an important feature that makes this piece unique.

Positioning the 2nd layer 90° to the base layer of glass

FS4 - Contour Fuse Schedule

Segment Description	Segment Number	Ramp Rate Degree Per Hour	Final Target Temperature	Hold-Soak Minutes
Primary Heat & Bubble Soak	1	800°F - 435°C	1150°F - 635°C	30
Intention Heat & Target Soak	2	300°F - 165°C	1370°F - 745°C	10
Rapid Drop to Anneal Soak	3	AFAP Full or 9999	950°F - 510°C	45
Slow Descent Anneal Cool	4	125°F - 67°C	700°F - 370°C	0
Power-off Cool to Room Temp	5	0000 Kiln Off	75°F - 25°C Room Temp	Do Not Open Kiln

The final step is to place the contour fused oval blank on my prepared ceramic mold then set my controller to the **MF1 - Mold Forming** schedule below. Then close the lid and turn the kiln on.

Flat blank still in the kiln after contour fuse firing,

MF1 - Mold Forming Schedule

Segment Description	Segment Number	Ramp Rate Degree Per Hour	Final Target Temperature	Hold-Soak Minutes
Primary Heat & Balance Soak	1	340°F - 185°C	1000°F - 540°C	10
Intention Heat & Target Soak	2	300°F - 165°C	1260°F - 682°C	10
Rapid Drop to Anneal Soak	3	AFAP Full or 9999	950°F - 510°C	45
Slow Descent Anneal Cool	4	125°F - 67°C	700°F - 370°C	0
Power-off Cool to Room Temp	5	0000 Kiln Off	75°F - 25°C Room Temp	Do Not Open Kiln

This latticework or basket weave design style is an exceptionally versatile design technique. It is really quite simple to do but the outcome gives the impression of complexity. This style can be the basis for dozens of different project designs and that is why I keep an assortment of pre-cut strips on hand at all times in clear and cathedral colors (see page 38).

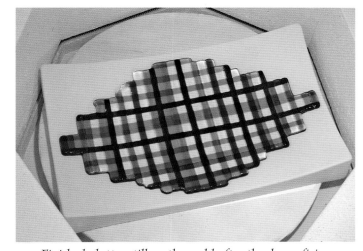

Finished platter still on the mold after the slump firing

Basket Weave Plate

Project at a Glance

Finished Project Size:
- 8" x 8" x 1" - 20 x 20 x 2.5 cm

Mold: Ceramic
- 9 1/4" square - 24 cm, sushi style

Kiln Firings: 2 Total
- FS6 - Deep Fuse
- MF1 - Mold Forming

Glass & Components:
- Border: clear (base) & med blue iridized cathedral (top)
- Inside Field: 2 layers of narrow strips in clear & cathedral colors

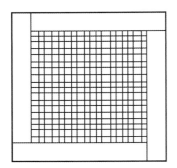

This simple and elegant project uses narrow cathedral strips in a basket weave pattern. After creating the blue iridized border, the rest of the project literally falls in place.

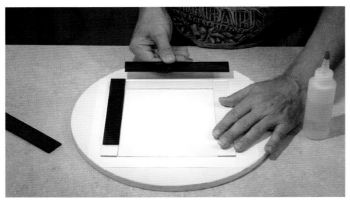

Clear border strips placed first then blue iridized layer on top

The border is 4 clear strips and 4 iridized cobalt blue cathedral strips, all cut to the same size of 1" x 7" - 2.5 cm x 17.5 cm. I placed a sheet of thin resist paper on my shelf. Then laid the clear strips in a pinwheel pattern for the bottom layer with the iridized blue strips on top, reversing the pinwheel corner pattern. I could have placed the iridized blue on the bottom (irid side up) with the clear on top and that would have added a gloss to the border. Then I secured the pieces with fusing glue. Since I don't have a layout drawing under my border assembly, I'll use a drafting square to make sure the square is actually square.

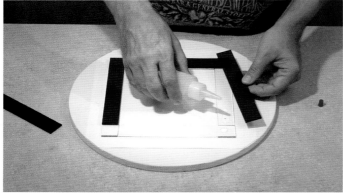

The blue border layer must overlap the clear in the corners

Checking the assembly to make sure it is a square, square

Basket Weave Plate

The glass strips for the inside basket weave pattern needed to be 6" - 15 cm long. I gathered an assortment of clear and light to medium colored cathedral strips and trimmed approximately 50 pieces to 6" - 15 cm long using my portable jig system (see this process in action on page 44, bottom right). Then I washed all the strips by soaking and agitating in my wash tub.

Now I can place the first layer of strips inside the border, swapping out widths as necessary until I get an ideal fit. There is no need to get too 'uptight' trying to get all the pieces 'up-tight'. I'm going to take this plate to a deep fuse and at that temperature all spaces will get filled in nicely. When I'm satisfied with the mix for the fist layer, I position the second layer 90° to the first to create the customary basket weave pattern.

Since this plate is intended for food service I want it to have a flat smooth top surface so I choose the **FS6 - Deep Fuse** schedule. The ramp rate chart (on page 23) says I can heat this first firing at 700°F - 380°C because the components are relatively small. I set my digital controller to the schedule below and fired it up.

Laying down the first strips, using a 1/3 clear to 2/3 color ratio

The second layer of strips are added at 90° to the bottom layer

FS6 - Deep Fuse Schedule

Segment Description	Segment Number	Ramp Rate Degree Per Hour	Final Target Temperature	Hold-Soak Minutes
Primary Heat & Bubble Soak	1	700°F - 380°C	1150°F - 635°C	30
Intention Heat & Target Soak	2	300°F - 165°C	1470°F - 800°C	10
Rapid Drop to Anneal Soak	3	AFAP Full or 9999	950°F - 510°C	45
Slow Descent Anneal Cool	4	125°F - 67°C	700°F - 370°C	0
Power-off Cool to Room Temp	5	0000 Kiln Off	75°F - 25°C Room Temp	Do Not Open Kiln

The next day I placed the flat blank on my square subtle-sloping plate mold (sushi style) and fired it using this **MF1 - Mold Forming** schedule with a ramp rate of 360°F - 195°C.

The assembly is placed in the kiln for a deep fuse firing

MF1 - Mold Forming Schedule

Segment Description	Segment Number	Ramp Rate Degree Per Hour	Final Target Temperature	Hold-Soak Minutes
Primary Heat & Balance Soak	1	360°F - 195°C	1000°F - 540°C	10
Intention Heat & Target Soak	2	300°F -165°C	1260°F - 682°C	10
Rapid Drop to Anneal Soak	3	AFAP Full or 9999	950°F - 510°C	45
Slow Descent Anneal Cool	4	125°F - 67°C	700°F - 370°C	0
Power-off Cool to Room Temp	5	0000 Kiln Off	75°F - 25°C Room Temp	Do Not Open Kiln

Center the fused blank on the mold ready for a slump firing

A Platter On-Edge

Project at a Glance

Finished Project Size:
- 6 3/4" x 9" x 1" - 17 x 23 x 2.5 cm

Mold: Ceramic
- 7 1/2" x 12 1/2" - 19 x 32 cm rectangle, sushi style

Kiln Firings: 2 Total
- FS3 - Texture Fuse
- MF1 - Mold Forming

Glass & Components:
- Border: clear (base) & black iridized cathedral (top)
- Inside Field: 1 layer of narrow strips (on edge) in clear & cathedral colors

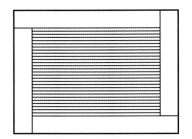

This striking platter uses glass strips stacked on edge across the center. It was fired to a Texture Fuse level to produce a delightfully tactile surface.

The clear border strips are placed on a sheet of thin resist paper

I created the 1" - 2.5 cm border with clear strips on the bottom and black iridized strips on top. The border strips were 6" and 8" - 15 and 20 cm. I placed thin resist paper on my shelf then placed the border pieces in the center using a pinwheel pattern (reversed pinwheel for the top layer) and secured it with glue.

I calculated that I would need about 40 to 43 strips for the inside field (8 per inch - 10 per 3 cm) so I gathered an assortment of clear and colored cathedral strips from my stash (see page 39 bottom) and used my portable jig system to trim them to exactly 7" - 17.5 cm long.

The black border pieces are placed to overlap the clear

Using the jig system to score all strips the same length

A Platter On-Edge

The glass strips need to be cleaned before they are placed in the design. I put them in my washtub to soak then take them out and pat dry on a terry towel.

Now I'll stack the strips on edge inside my border frame. I used mostly light colored strips for this project because I did not want the plate to be too dark. Although I tried to make sure all pieces were exactly the same length, some needed a little grinding to fit and some were a little short, creating a gap. I knew some of these gaps would open up during fusing, resulting in a few open spaces between the strip ends and the border, but for me these open spaces add texture and interest to the piece.

This is a decorative piece (not intended for serving) and I wanted the surface to have an irregular undulating look and feel. I set my controller to the **FS3 - Texture Fuse** schedule with a primary heat ramp of 700°F - 380°C, because the components are relatively small. Then fired the kiln.

Placing the narrow strips 'on edge' inside the border

FS3 - Texture Fuse Schedule

Segment Description	Seg Number	Ramp Rate Degree Per Hour	Final Target Temperature	Hold-Soak Minutes
Primary Heat & Bubble Soak	1	700°F - 380°C	1150°F - 635°C	30
Intention Heat & Target Soak	2	300°F - 165°C	1330°F - 720°C	10
Rapid Drop to Anneal Soak	3	AFAP Full or 9999	950°F - 510°C	45
Slow Descent Anneal Cool	4	125°F - 67°C	700°F - 370°C	0
Power-off Cool to Room Temp	5	0000 Kiln Off	75°F - 25°C Room Temp	Do Not Open Kiln

Strip placement is complete and ready for the fuse firing

The next day when I opened the kiln, I was thrilled with the surface texture and interesting color mix. I placed the flat blank on my rectangle 'sushi style' mold then set an **MF1 - Mold Forming** schedule. I checked the ramp rate chart on page 23 for a 64 SqIn - 20 SqCm blank and used the suggested 360°F - 195°C to set my controller. Then turned on the kiln.

Fused blank is centered on the mold ready for slump firing

MF1 - Mold Forming Schedule

Segment Description	Segment Number	Ramp Rate Degree Per Hour	Final Target Temperature	Hold-Soak Minutes
Primary Heat & Balance Soak	1	360°F - 195°C	1000°F - 540°C	10
Intention Heat & Target Soak	2	300°F - 165°C	1260°F - 682°C	10
Rapid Drop to Anneal Soak	3	AFAP Full or 9999	950°F - 510°C	45
Slow Descent Anneal Cool	4	125°F - 67°C	700°F - 370°C	0
Power-off Cool to Room Temp	5	0000 Kiln Off	75°F - 25°C Room Temp	Do Not Open Kiln

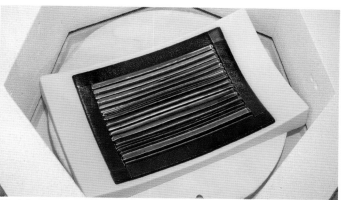

Finished piece still on the mold in the kiln after the slump firing

Tutorial - Sculptural Stringers

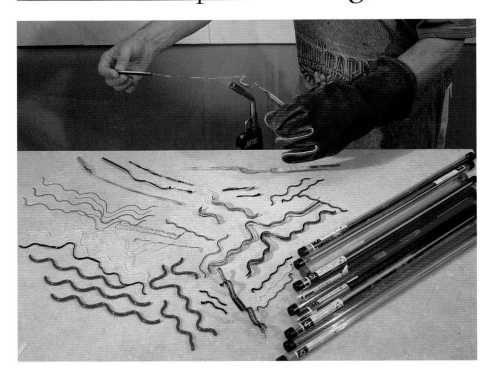

An absent minded pencil sketch is known as a doodle - really nothing more than a bunch of swirls, squiggles, zigzags, and other fun shapes. Sculptural stringers can be thought of as glass doodles - intriguing design components that can be incorporated into abstract, contemporary, floral, and landscape designs.

It is easier than you might think to create these glass doodle shapes. All you need is an ordinary candle, a propane torch or a shape mold in your kiln to create some truly remarkable glass designs.

Stringers, noodles and pre-shaped components

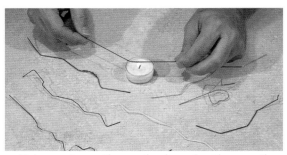

Stringers & noodles can be shaped with a candle

Ceramic molds can be used to shape components

I have an interesting collection of stringers, rods, swizzels, zigzags, whoosits, and whatcamacallits in assorted colors. It seems every time I visit my fused glass supplier I come away with 1 or 2 more 'tubes of intrigue.' That's because stringers, noodles and other pre-shaped components are so versatile. The assortment is awesome and many of them can be used exactly as they are purchased. The photo at left shows a variety of purchased items including some water-jet cut designs (in the foreground) that would be very difficult to make on your own.

We are not limited to using these components right out of the box, we can reshape them to meet our design needs. One of the easiest ways to shape spaghetti stringers is with an ordinary candle. Hold the stringer horizontally over the candle flame for about 8 seconds and it will soften enough to bend it. If you hold the stringer steady in one location you can bend it at a sharp angle. However, if you move it slowly back and forth through the flame you can coax a gentle curve. It's easy, a lot of fun to do and you'll be amazed at the variety of shapes that you can create.

Another way to shape stringers is by using a ceramic mold. I have a wave mold with 3 ridges and 4 valleys that I use to create multicolored spaghetti ribbons that contain 8 stringers in each group. Sometimes I'll use these ribbons as a complete unit (see page 48) and other times I'll separate them into bits and pieces to be incorporated into my design. I used this same mold to shape the red glass rods shown in the photo at the top of this page and also used it in the Tidal Pool Plate project on page 50.

It is not always necessary to have a specific mold for creating shapes. Many times an ordinary mold for bowls, plates or frit casting can be adapted to create stringer shapes. Another idea is to use an assortment of kiln components such as risers, shelf supports, firebrick pieces, and fiberboard. Remember to coat these with kiln wash before using them as shape molds.

I have a stainless steel pipe forming kit that is made specifically for component shaping. These pipes are arranged on a kiln shelf, using kiln risers and fiberboard spacers to form a variety of shapes. You can shape 20 to 50 stringers in a single firing and it doesn't take long. These components are so thin they can be ramped up at full speed (I ramp at 900° F - 500°C) and as soon as they have reached the forming temperature of 1260°F - 680°C the kiln can be shut off and allowed to cool with the lid closed.

If you have ever tried your hand at bead making you will be familiar with the process of using a torch to heat and shape glass. All you need is a small bead torch or an ordinary propane torch and you'll be bending and shaping strips of fusing glass to make your own stringers, multi colored twists, crazy shapes and all sorts of entertaining stuff (see photo at right and on previous page at top). Sometimes I'll sit at my bench with a torch for couple of hours to bend and twist strips of fusing glass - just for fun. But before trying this at home you must have the proper safety equipment. You'll need high temperature gloves, didymium coated eyeglasses, a heat resistant pad for your bench and a piece of fiber blanket to wrap your hot components and allow them cool slowly. I collect all my shapes and store them in a container drawer for future use. Remember it's very important to mark the COE number of the glass on the container because there is no way to tell later. If you use the wrong COE component in one of your pieces it will cause trouble.

One of my favorite ways to make incredible stringers, curlicues and loop-d-loops and all manner of sculptural stringers is to use a vitrigraph kiln. If you have never heard of one before it's basically a small kiln with a hole drilled in the center of the floor. A crucible (4 inch terra-cotta planter pot) is placed over the hole and filled with fusible glass shards. The kiln is mounted on a 48" - 1.2 m high metal shelf to permit access under the kiln. The kiln is heated to a high melt temperature around 1700°F - 930°C until the glass begins to slowly emerge through the hole in the bottom of the kiln. This is when the fun begins. You carefully grab the hot glass with tweezers (wearing all the necessary safety equipment of course) to pull and twist and guide the glass stringer as it emerges from the kiln. If you're interested in building one of these kilns for yourself all you need is a small tabletop jewelry kiln (the type where the floor is not attached) and a piece of fiberboard large enough to replace the bottom floor of the kiln. You will find an entire chapter on how to build and use a vitrigraph kiln in Petra Kaiser's book 'Fuse It' by Wardell Publications - www.wardellpublications.com

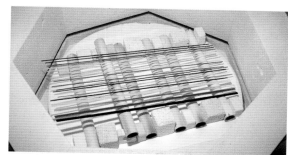

The stainless steel pipe forming kit ready to go

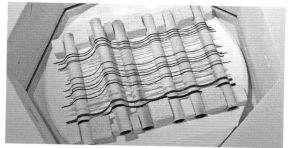

Shaped stringers after firing on the SS pipe kit

Contrasting narrow strips were heated then twisted

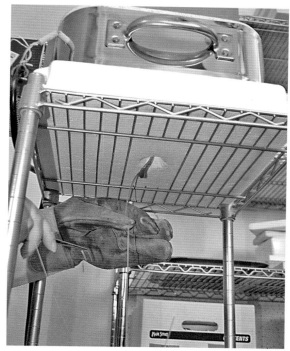

Petra Kaiser's vitrigraph kiln from her book 'Fuse It' by Wardell Publications. The hot glass is shaped and guided as it emerges from the bottom of the kiln.

Hanging by a Thread

Project at a Glance

Finished Project Size:
- 9" square x 1 5/8" - 23 cm x 4 cm

Mold: Ceramic
- 9 1/4" - 24 cm square, sushi style

Kiln Firings: 3 Total
- SCS - Small Component
- FS1 - Elevated Tack
- MF1 - Mold Forming

Glass & Components:
- Base Layer: black opal
- Design Layer: spaghetti stringers 8 per row in assorted colors; & clear iridized chunk frit

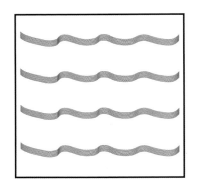

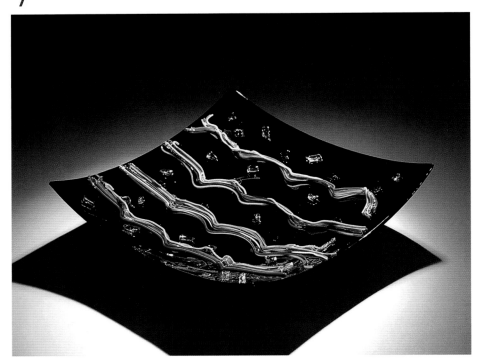

There is something magical about the way these stringers seem to be gently resting on the shiny black background, appearing as if they were cotton threads of vibrant colors, freshly dyed and lovingly placed there to dry.

I had just received my ceramic waveform mold and I wanted to give it a try. I went to my collection of spaghetti stringers and put together 4 bundles of 8 stringers each, using the brightest colors I had. I cut them to the full length of the mold, hoping that the ends would droop and branch out in interesting ways. Then I clumped them very tightly together on the mold so the stringers in each bundle would tack together to form a single fused bundle.

I placed the mold and stringer assembly into my kiln and fired them using the **SCS - Small Component Shaping** schedule.

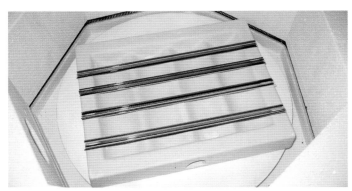

Spaghetti stringers placed on the waveform mold

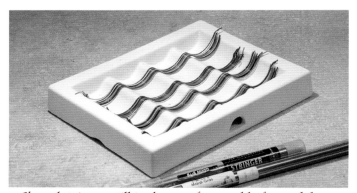

Shaped stringers still in the waveform mold after cool down

SCS - Small Component Shaping Schedule

Segment Description	Segment Number	Ramp Rate Degree Per Hour	Final Target Temperature	Hold-Soak Minutes
Intention Heat Target Soak	1	900°F - 495°C	1245°F - 675°C	10
Power-off Cool to Room Temp	2	0000 Kiln Off	75°F - 25°C Room Temp	Do Not Open Kiln

Hanging by a Thread

This piece was intentionally created to be a decorative object for display only, so a single layer of smooth black opal glass would be plenty. My plan was to slump it into my square 'sushi style' mold and I know that it can handle a 9" - 23 cm blank. I cut the black opal then smoothed and slightly beveled the edge with an extra fine 'Fusing' grinder bit, being careful not to round off the corners.

I placed the stringer bundles on the base glass parallel and equally spaced. Then I used chunks of clear iridized to tilt each bundle slightly in an attempt to encourage the stringers to twist and distort as they fell over during the slump firing.

I wanted the stringer bundles to appear as if they were floating on the surface, so I set my controller to an **FS1 - Elevated Tack** schedule and fired it.

Positioning the spaghetti stringers on the black base glass

FS1 - Elevated Tack Schedule

Segment Description	Segment Number	Ramp Rate Degree Per Hour	Final Target Temperature	Hold-Soak Minutes
Primary Heat & Bubble Soak	1	400°F - 220°C	1150°F - 635°C	30
Intention Heat & Target Soak	2	300°F - 165°C	1245°F - 675°C	10
Rapid Drop to Anneal Soak	3	AFAP Full or 9999	950°F - 510°C	45
Slow Descent Anneal Cool	4	125°F - 67°C	700°F - 370°C	0
Power-off Cool to Room Temp	5	0000 Kiln Off	75°F - 25°C Room Temp	Do Not Open Kiln

The tack firing turned out fantastic but the clear chunks were left isolated after the stringer ribbons twisted over. I decided to resolve that problem by adding even more clear iridized chunks, strategically placed to balance the design. These will easily tack to the black base during the slump firing.

I placed the tack fused blank on my square 'sushi style' plate mold, then positioned the additional clear iridescent chunks. I set my controller to the **MF1 - Mold Forming** schedule - modified to have only a 1 minute soak at target temperature.

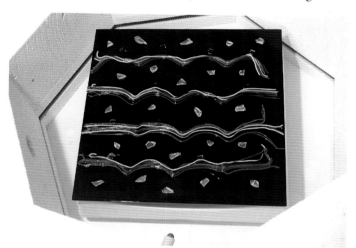

Tack fused assembly with additional clear frit on the mold

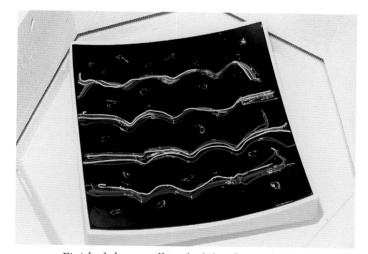

Finished slump still in the kiln after cool down

MF1 - Mold Forming Schedule

Segment Description	Segment Number	Ramp Rate Degree Per Hour	Final Target Temperature	Hold-Soak Minutes
Primary Heat & Balance Soak	1	360°F - 195°C	1000°F - 540°C	10
Intention Heat & Target Soak	2	300°F - 165°C	1260°F - 682°C	1
Rapid Drop to Anneal Soak	3	AFAP Full or 9999	950°F - 510°C	45
Slow Descent Anneal Cool	4	125°F - 67°C	700°F - 370°C	0
Power-off Cool to Room Temp	5	0000 Kiln Off	75°F - 25°C Room Temp	Do Not Open Kiln

Tidal Pool Plate

Project at a Glance

Finished Project Size:
- 9" square x 1 5/8" - 23 cm x 4 cm

Mold: Ceramic
- 9 1/4" - 24 cm square, sushi style

Kiln Firings: 3 Total
- SCS - Small Component
- FS6 - Deep Fuse
- MF1 - Mold Forming

Glass & Components:
- Base Layer: clear
- 2nd layer: clear with black streamers; red opal border
- Design layer: red opal rods 5 mm, black frit balls

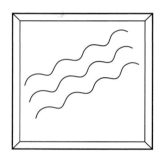

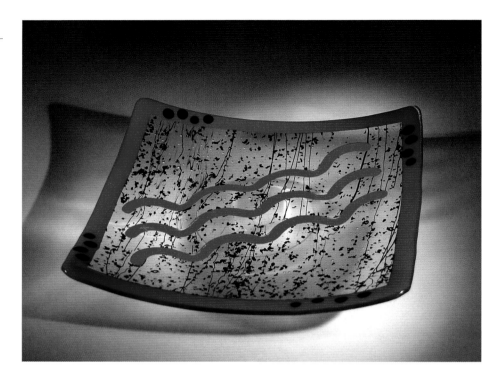

These three parallel wavy lines remind me of the international sign for water, while the black pebbles and streamers in clear remind me of a tidal pool full of tiny sea creatures.

The inspiration for this plate came when I purchased a handful of hot red opal rods that are 3/16" - 5 mm diameter and 16" - 40 cm long. I decided to cut 3 of them in half and then shape those 6 pieces in my wave mold using the **SCS - Small Component Shaping** schedule below.

The rods have been placed in the wave mold

SCS - Small Component Shaping Schedule				
Segment Description	Segment Number	Ramp Rate Degree Per Hour	Final Target Temp °F-°C	Hold-Soak Minutes
Intention Heat Target Soak	1	900°F - 495°C	1245°F - 675°C	10
Power-off Cool to Room Temp	2	0000 Kiln Off	75°F - 25°C Room Temp	Do Not Open Kiln

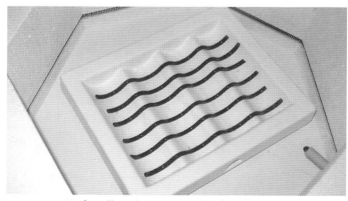

Rods still in the wave mold after slumping

Assembly begins on the 2nd layer

Tidal Pool Plate Project 8

I wanted to slump this plate on my 9 1/4" - 24 cm square 'sushi style' mold so I cut my clear base 9" - 23 cm square. Then I cut the 1/2" - 15 mm border strips from a red opal glass. The next piece to cut was the clear with black streamers that needed to be 8" - 20 cm square for the central field.

I cleaned all the components, including my wavy rods, then assembled them according to my plan. After a review, I felt the borders needed something more. So I raided my component drawers and found a stash of black frit balls that I had made long ago. I placed 4 of them in each corner and the design was complete. I loaded the assembly into my kiln and fired it according to the **FS6 - Deep Fuse** schedule.

Positioning the borders, field glass & rods on the base glass

FS6 - Deep Fuse Schedule

Segment Description	Segment Number	Ramp Rate Degree Per Hour	Final Target Temperature	Hold-Soak Minutes
Primary Heat & Bubble Soak	1	400°F - 220°C	1150°F - 635°C	30
Intention Heat & Target Soak	2	300°F - 165°C	1470°F - 800°C	10
Rapid Drop to Anneal Soak	3	AFAP Full or 9999	950°F - 510°C	45
Slow Descent Anneal Cool	4	125°F - 67°C	700°F - 370°C	0
Power-off Cool to Room Temp	5	0000 Kiln Off	75°F - 25°C Room Temp	Do Not Open Kiln

The next day after it had cooled completely I placed the full-fused flat blank on my square 'sushi style' plate mold then set my controller to the standard **MF1 - Mold Forming** schedule on page 35 - using an initial ramp rate of 340°F - 185°C (taken from the Ramp Rate Chart on page 23). Then turned the kiln on.

Pre-fuse assembly ready to go into the kiln for full fuse firing

MF1 - Mold Forming Schedule

Segment Description	Segment Number	Ramp Rate Degree Per Hour	Final Target Temperature	Hold-Soak Minutes
Primary Heat & Balance Soak	1	340°F - 185°C	1000°F - 540°C	10
Intention Heat & Target Soak	2	300°F - 165°C	1260°F - 682°C	10
Rapid Drop to Anneal Soak	3	AFAP Full or 9999	950°F - 510°C	45
Slow Descent Anneal Cool	4	125°F - 67°C	700°F - 370°C	0
Power-off Cool to Room Temp	5	0000 Kiln Off	75°F - 25°C Room Temp	Do Not Open Kiln

Fused blank in the kiln & on the mold, ready for slump firing

Oscillation Plate

Project at a Glance

Finished Project Size:
- 11 1/2" diameter x 1 1/4"
  - 29 cm diameter x 3 cm

Mold: Ceramic
- 12 1/2" - 32 cm diameter round with 24 accordion pleats

Kiln Firings: 3 Total
- SCS - Small Component
- FS5 - Full Fuse
- MF1 - Mold Forming

Glass & Components:
- Base Layer: clear
- 2nd Layer: green cathedral
- Design Layer: shaped spaghetti stringers in assorted colors

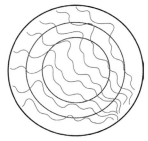

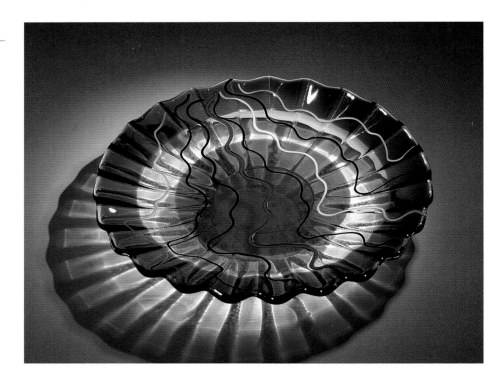

I love the way the oscillating spaghetti stringers slash across the concentric circles. They bring some visual relief to an otherwise monotonous repetition of circles and pleats.

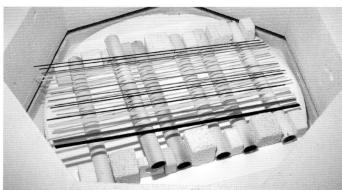

Stainless steel pipe forming setup before shape firing

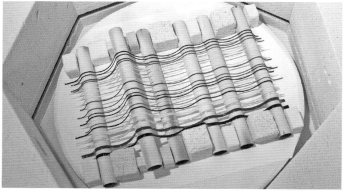

Stainless steel pipe forming setup after shape firing (see page 47)

The first step is to create the oscillating spaghetti stringers. This is accomplished using a stainless steel pipe forming set up in my kiln (see page 47 for more details) to shape a combination of spaghetti and fettuccine stringers in red, white & black. I fired them using the **SCS - Small Component Shaping** schedule.

SCS - Small Component Shaping Schedule				
Segment Description	Seg Number	Ramp Rate Degree Per Hour	Final Target Temp °F-°C	Hold-Soak Minutes
Intention Heat Target Soak	1	900°F - 495°C	1245°F - 675°C	10
Power-off Cool to Room Temp	2	0000 Kiln Off	75°F - 25°C Room Temp	Do Not Open Kiln

The next step is to cut the components to make the flat blank. I used my swing arm circle cutter to score and break a 12" - 30 cm disk of clear glass and also to make a 6" -15 cm green cathedral disk. Then I created a paper template for the 1 1/2" - 4 cm wide outside border. I find it so much easier to have a paper pattern to trace the border sections onto the glass and then follow the traced lines with my glasscutter to score and break the glass.

Oscillation Plate Project 9

For this project I cut my border into 4 sections but the border would have worked cut into 6 or 8 sections. In fact border pieces that have a smaller radius are a little easier to cut (the inside score is not as severe) and they also allow a more efficient use of glass.

The central clear ring does not have a 2nd layer, it is the base clear glass only (1 layer thick only). The components were cleaned, assembled and placed in the kiln. I fired it to **FS5 - Full Fuse** schedule and used the suggested Ramp Rate for a 'large single thick initial firing' taken from the chart on page 23.

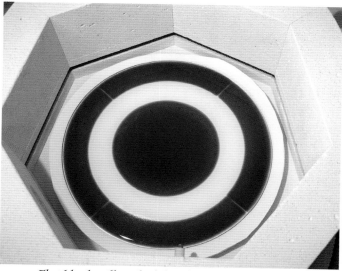

Flat blank still in the kiln after the full fuse firing

FS5 - Full Fuse Schedule				
Segment Description	Segment Number	Ramp Rate Degree Per Hour	Final Target Temperature	Hold-Soak Minutes
Primary Heat & Bubble Soak	1	350°F - 190°C	1150°F - 635°C	30
Intention Heat & Target Soak	2	300°F - 165°C	1425°F - 775°C	10
Rapid Drop to Anneal Soak	3	AFAP Full or 9999	950°F - 510°C	45
Slow Descent Anneal Cool	4	125°F - 67°C	700°F - 370°C	0
Power-off Cool to Room Temp	5	0000 Kiln Off	75°F - 25°C Room Temp	Do Not Open Kiln

The next step is to add the oscillating spaghetti stringers. I tried various configurations and color combinations then settled on using 8 stringers in a fan-out pattern. Trimmed using mosaic nippers.

I wanted the stringers to be elevated slightly, as they would be if I used an elevated tack schedule. I decided that I could combine the tack fuse and the slump into one firing simply by increasing the final target temperature of the **MF1 - Mold Forming** schedule to 1280°F - 695°C and extending the hold time to 45 minutes. This modification will easily tack the stringers and will enable the glass to slump more fully into the deep pleats of this mold. So I set my controller to the modified Dimensional Tack & Mold Forming schedule shown below. Then fired the kiln.

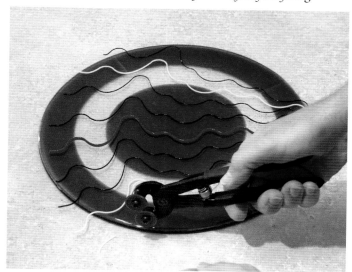

Trimming & positioning stringers on the full fused blank

MF1 - Mold Forming Schedule				
Segment Description	Segment Number	Ramp Rate Degree Per Hour	Final Target Temperature	Hold-Soak Minutes
Primary Heat & Balance Soak	1	320°F - 175°C	1000°F - 540°C	10
Intention Heat & Target Soak	2	300°F - 165°C	1280°F - 695°C	45
Rapid Drop to Anneal Soak	3	AFAP Full or 9999	950°F - 510°C	45
Slow Descent Anneal Cool	4	125°F - 67°C	700°F - 370°C	0
Power-off Cool to Room Temp	5	0000 Kiln Off	75°F - 25°C Room Temp	Do Not Open Kiln

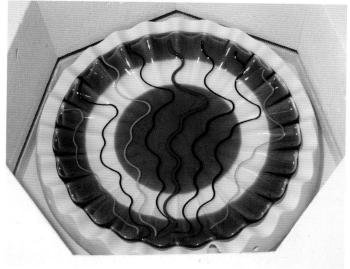

Finished plate still on the mold after the tack/slump firing

Squaresville Sushi Set

Project at a Glance

Finished Project Sizes:
- 7" x 12" x 1 1/4" - 18 x 30 x 3 cm
- 4 3/4" sqr x 1" - 12 cm sqr x 2.5 cm

Molds: Ceramic (x 2)
- 7 1/2" x 12 1/2" - 19 x 32 cm rectangle, sushi style
- 6" - 15 cm square, sushi style

Kiln Firings: 2 Total
- FS6 - Deep Fuse
- MF1 - Mold Forming

Glass & Components:
- Base Layer: clear
- 2nd Layer: white, med blue, steel blue & leaf green opal
- Design Layer: med blue & green

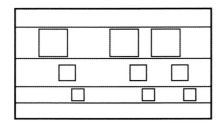

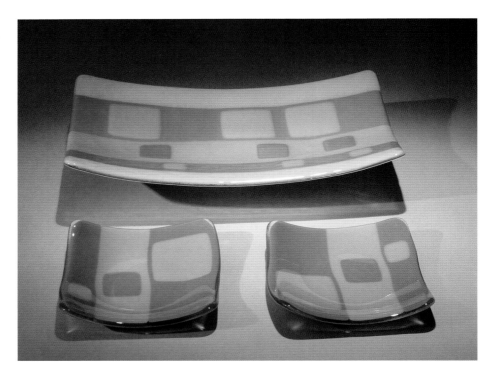

I wanted to create a "Sushi Set for Two" with the traditional long and narrow serving boat and two matching side plates. I purposely kept the design straightforward and understated to allow the sushi roll pieces to be the megastars when the dish is served.

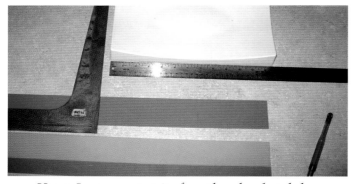

Use an L-square cut strips from the colored opal glass

I measured both of the molds to determine the base glass sizes. I like to make an allowance of at least 1/4" - 5 mm on all sides to ensure the flat blank is slightly smaller than the overall dimension of molds. I'll make the base glass for the rectangle serving boat 7" x 12" - 18 x 30 cm and I'll make the base glass for the side plates 4 3/4" - 12 cm square. I cut all 3 base pieces from smooth clear glass then used an extra-fine Fusing bit on my grinder to round the corners slightly. I cleaned them and set them aside.

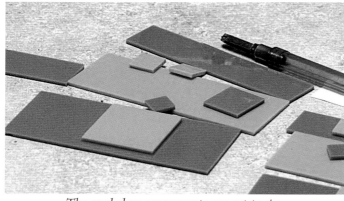

The opal glass components are cut to size

Preliminary layout to check the sizes and refine the fit

Next I used my L-square to cut some strips from the opal glass colors as follows: White opal: 1" - 2.5 cm and 1 1/4" - 3.5 cm; Medium blue opal: 2" - 5 cm; Steel blue opal: 1" - 2.5 cm; Leaf green opal: 1 3/4" - 4.5 cm and 3/4" - 2 cm

I trimmed the strips to length for the serving boat (12" - 30 cm) and both side plates (4 3/4" - 12 cm) for the 2nd layer, by following the pattern drawing layout. Then I cut the squares for the design layer from the same strips. I arranged the glass pieces on my bench to do a preliminary layout to check the fit and sizes. I made some adjustments using the Fusing bit on my grinder and rounded the corner pieces on the second layer to match the base. Then I cleaned all the glass.

I placed a sheet of thin resist paper on the kiln shelf then arranged the pieces for the serving boat rectangle. I placed the assembly in my kiln and fired it according to the **FS6 - Deep Fuse** Schedule below. When the kiln had cooled to room temperature, I removed the rectangle and placed both side plate blanks on the kiln shelf and fired those using the same **FS6 - Deep Fuse** Schedule. (Note: You could ramp these up a little faster, consult the ramp rate chart on page 23.)

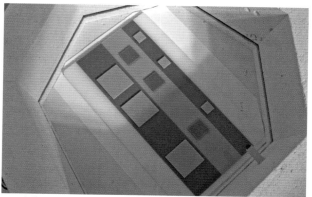

The rectangle serving boat assembly is ready to be fused

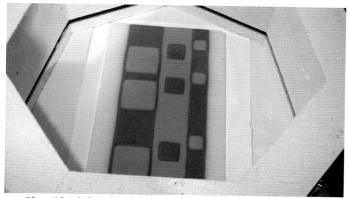

Glass blank has been fired to an FS6 - Deep Fuse schedule

FS6 - Deep Fuse Schedule

Segment Description	Segment Number	Ramp Rate Degree Per Hour	Final Target Temperature	Hold-Soak Minutes
Primary Heat & Bubble Soak	1	400°F - 220°C	1150°F - 635°C	30
Intention Heat & Target Soak	2	300°F - 165°C	1470°F - 800°C	10
Rapid Drop to Anneal Soak	3	AFAP Full or 9999	950°F - 510°C	45
Slow Descent Anneal Cool	4	125°F - 67°C	700°F - 370°C	0
Power-off Cool to Room Temp	5	0000 Kiln Off	75°F - 25°C Room Temp	Do Not Open Kiln

The final step was to place the flat fuse blanks on their respective molds and fired them, one at a time, using the **MF1 - Mold Forming** schedule below.

Fused blank is centered on the mold ready for slump firing

MF1 - Mold Forming Schedule

Segment Description	Segment Number	Ramp Rate Degree Per Hour	Final Target Temperature	Hold-Soak Minutes
Primary Heat & Bubble Soak	1	340°F - 185°C	1000°F - 540°C	10
Intention Heat & Target Soak	2	300°F - 165°C	1260°F - 682°C	10
Rapid Drop to Anneal Soak	3	AFAP Full or 9999	950°F - 510°C	45
Slow Descent Anneal Cool	4	125°F - 67°C	700°F - 370°C	0
Power-off Cool to Room Temp	5	0000 Kiln Off	75°F - 25°C Room Temp	Do Not Open Kiln

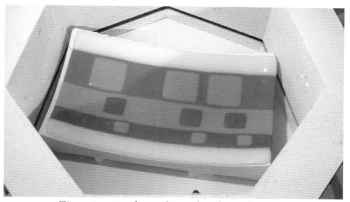

First piece in the sushi set has been slumped

The Wright Plate

Project at a Glance

Finished Project Size:
- 9" square x 1 5/8" - 23 cm x 4 cm

Mold: Ceramic
- 9 1/4" - 24 cm square, sushi style

Kiln Firings: 2 Total
- FS5 - Full Fuse
- MF1 - Mold Forming

Glass & Components:
- Base Layer: clear
- 2nd Layer: med blue opal
- Design Layer: white, leaf green & steel blue opal

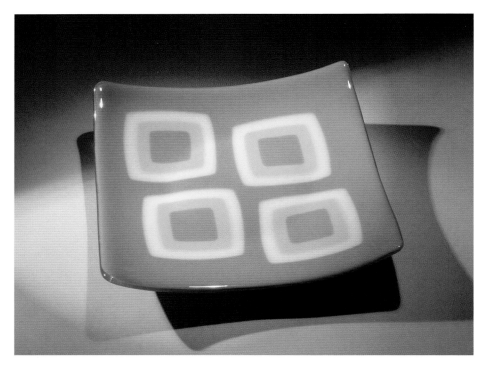

This serving plate uses the same colors as the sushi set in the previous project. The design is also similar but the blue background is the dominant feature here.

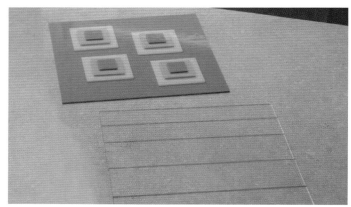

Squares stacked on 2nd layer, base layer in the foreground

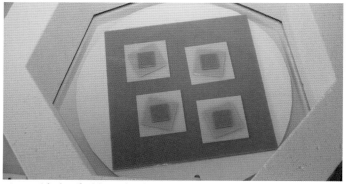

Assembly loaded but the design needs some creative adjustment

I measured the square sushi style mold and decided I could make a 9" - 23 cm square flat blank. I used my L-square to cut a piece of medium blue opal to this size and I will use that glass for the 2nd layer.

For the base layer I used some strips of clear that I had left over from a previous project (see foreground in photo at left). I trimmed these strips as necessary to make them into a 9" - 23 cm square. There are 2 advantages to using these strips for the base. One, of course, is that I get to use up some leftover smaller pieces of clear and that's always a good thing. But the more important reason is, having a multi-piece base reduces the incidence of bubbles forming between the base and 2nd layer. The space between the clear strips presents an ideal opportunity for the air to escape - especially if you are using thin resist paper . Compare this technique to the previous Squaresville sushi set project (page 54). Notice how the base layer in that project was a single piece of clear while the 2nd layer was made using strips of various colors. This is simply two different ways to achieve the same effect - an escape for the air.

The Wright Plate

Again, I used my L-square to cut some strips from the opal glass that I picked for the design layer. The strip widths were as follows:

White opal: 2 1/2" - 6.5 cm

Leaf green: 1 3/4" - 4.5 cm

Steel blue: 1" - 2.5 cm

Then I cut 4 squares from each color strip. I tried a couple of different configurations with the squares. The middle photo on the previous page shows the design with the squares parallel to one another while the photo directly below it shows the leaf green squares rotated slightly. I like both designs but after I placed the assembly in the kiln I decided to go with the all parallel squares because I thought it would a better match for the sushi set that I had created previously, so I adjusted the design.

Then I set the controller for an **FS5 - Full Fuse** schedule. I used the Med-Plus ramp rate speed that was listed in the 'Initial Firings' ramp chart on page 23. Then hit the switch to light up the kiln.

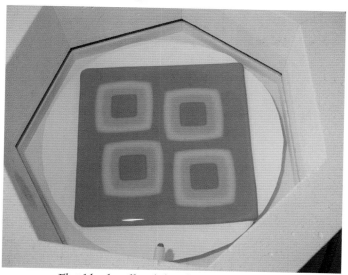

Flat blank still in kiln after deep fuse firing

FS5 - Full Fuse Schedule

Segment Description	Segment Number	Ramp Rate Degree Per Hour	Final Target Temperature	Hold-Soak Minutes
Primary Heat & Bubble Soak	1	400°F - 220°C	1150°F - 635°C	30
Intention Heat & Target Soak	2	300°F - 165°C	1425°F - 775°C	10
Rapid Drop to Anneal Soak	3	AFAP Full or 9999	950°F - 510°C	45
Slow Descent Anneal Cool	4	125°F - 67°C	700°F - 370°C	0
Power-off Cool to Room Temp	5	0000 Kiln Off	75°F - 25°C Room Temp	Do Not Open Kiln

Blank positioned on mold ready to be slump fired

The final step was to center the full fused blank on my prepared ceramic mold, place it in the kiln, then set my controller for the **MF1 - Mold Forming** schedule listed below and fire it.

MF1 - Mold Forming Schedule

Segment Description	Segment Number	Ramp Rate Degree Per Hour	Final Target Temperature	Hold-Soak Minutes
Primary Heat & Bubble Soak	1	340°F - 185°C	1000°F - 540°C	10
Intention Heat & Target Soak	2	300°F - 165°C	1260°F - 682°C	10
Rapid Drop to Anneal Soak	3	AFAP Full or 9999	950°F - 510°C	45
Slow Descent Anneal Cool	4	125°F - 67°C	700°F - 370°C	0
Power-off Cool to Room Temp	5	0000 Kiln Off	75°F - 25°C Room Temp	Do Not Open Kiln

Finished plate still on mold in kiln after slump firing

I Love You This Much

Project at a Glance

Finished Project Size:
- 9" square x 1/2" - 23 cm x 13 mm

Mold: Fiber Paper
- 2 pcs 10" x 1/8" - 26 cm x 3 mm

Kiln Firings: 2 Total
- 1 Fuse - FS5 - Full Fuse
- 1 Slump - MF1 - Mold Forming

Glass & Components:
- Base Layer: white opal
- 2nd Layer: iridized clear border strips, pink opal precut large heart
- Design Layer: precut hearts: 1 white opal & 2 pink opal

W hen a cartoon character falls in love they show his heart beating so hard that it is bursting out of his chest. That animation of a beating heart is what I was going for here.

The hearts I used for this project were purchased as precut fusible components and that made this is a very simple project to create. If you cannot find these precut hearts it is possible to create them yourself. Most of the heart is relatively easy to score & break but the deep V at the top is virtually impossible to get by scoring and breaking alone. If you have a diamond wire saw (i.e. Ringsaw) or a diamond bandsaw this would be a perfect opportunity to use it. Score and break the outside perimeter of the heart but do not try to score into the V, instead use your saw to complete this portion of the heart.

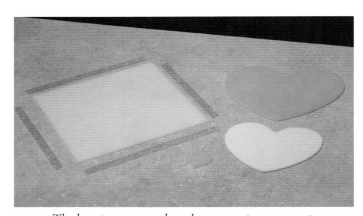

The hearts were purchased as pre-cut components

Assembly is complete and ready to be placed in kiln

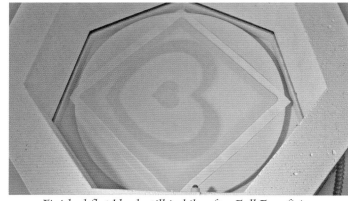

Finished flat blank still in kiln after Full Fuse firing

I Love You This Much

Another option would be to score into the V as deep as you can then use your grinder to finish it. A 3rd possibility (and the one that I prefer) is to design the hearts as two pieces of glass by forming a gentle S-curve down the middle of each heart (see dashed line on the drawing). The S-curve makes scoring and breaking very easy and the faint line it leaves on the fused piece creates the illusion of a rounded 3-D heart.

I assembled my glass starting with the white opal base then added the 1/2" - 1.5 cm wide clear border strips, then stacked the 3 hearts in the center. I placed the assembly in the kiln and set the controller for an **FS5 - Full Fuse** schedule and turned it on.

Tracing the outside perimeter onto two layers of fiber paper

FS5 - Full Fuse Schedule

Segment Description	Segment Number	Ramp Rate Degree Per Hour	Final Target Temperature	Hold-Soak Minutes
Primary Heat & Bubble Soak	1	400°F - 220°C	1150°F - 635°C	30
Intention Heat & Target Heat	2	300°F - 165°C	1425°F - 775°C	10
Rapid Drop to Anneal Soak	3	AFAP Full or 9999	950°F - 510°C	45
Slow Descent Anneal Cool	4	125°F - 67°C	700°F - 370°C	0
Power-off Cool to Room Temp	5	0000 Kiln Off	75°F - 25°C Room Temp	Do Not Open Kiln

Then I created the fiber paper mold to form the rim on this plate. I cut 2 pieces of 1/8" - 3 mm thick fiber paper, 10" - 26 cm square. I stacked these fiber paper pieces then placed my flat blank in the center and traced the outline. I measured 3/4" - 2 cm inside the traced line to make a border, then I used the lid from a frit jar (about 2" - 5 cm in dia) to draw a radius on the corners. I used a craft knife to cut through both layers of fiber paper following this new inside line.

3/4" - 2 cm allowance was made then fiber paper mold was cut

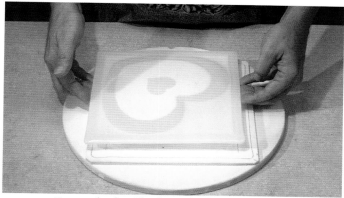

Center the flat blank on the fiber paper mold

Now I placed the double-thick fiber paper mold on a prepared kiln shelf then center the fused blank using the outside trace lines that I created earlier (clever don't you think?). I placed the assembly in my kiln and set the controller for an **MF1 - Mold Forming** schedule and fired it up.

MF1 - Mold Forming Schedule

Segment Description	Segment Number	Ramp Rate Degree Per Hour	Final Target Temperature	Hold-Soak Minutes
Primary Heat & Bubble Soak	1	340°F - 185°C	1000°F - 540°C	10
Intention Heat & Target Soak	2	300°F /-165°C	1260°F - 682°C	10
Rapid Drop to Anneal Soak	3	AFAP Full or 9999	950°F - 510°C	45
Slow Descent Anneal Cool	4	125°F - 67°C	700°F - 370°C	0
Power-off Cool to Room Temp	5	0000 Kiln Off	75°F - 25°C Room Temp	Do Not Open Kiln

Finished piece in the kiln after the slump firing

Isaac's Comet Tray

Project at a Glance

Finished Project Size:
- 9 1/4" x 6" x 1/2"
  - 23.5 x 15 x 13 mm

Mold: Fiber Paper 1/8" - 3 mm
- 2 pcs 10" x 7" - 26 cm x 18

Kiln Firings: 2 total
- FS3 - Texture Fuse
- MF1 - Mold Forming

Glass & Components:
- Base Layer: smooth clear
- 2nd Layer: black, lt blue & celery green opal; lt blue, lt green & med green cathedral
- Design Layer: spaghetti stringers (asstd colors), dichroic on clear fettuccine, yellow & red fine frit

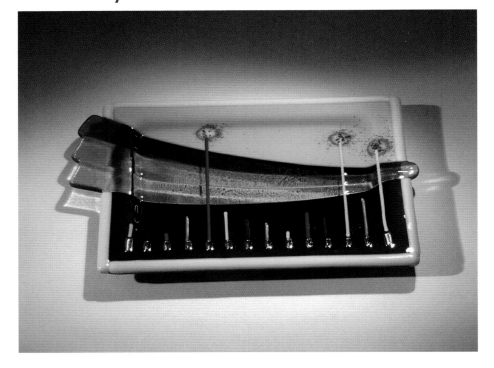

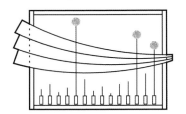

The idea for this design came while I was watching an Isaac Asimov 'Cosmos' documentary. You didn't really need to know that but I'm hoping an Asimov reference raises the cerebral value.

This project requires a paper template because the components must fit together accurately. Make 2 copies of the pattern (you can download it from www.joyoffusing.com) then cut one copy into pattern templates and save the other for the assembly. I used an L-square to cut the clear base rectangle 8" x 6" - 20 x 15 cm. Then I cut the clear support tabs that will be placed under both ends of the comet trail (see close-up image of similar support tabs on page 37 top right photo). Next I traced my patterns and cut the glass for the 2nd layer. I used my portable glass shop to cut the 1/4" - 6 mm narrow border strips (see page 39).

Paper template is created & cut to be used for glass patterns

Pattern is traced onto the glass to follow with glass cutter

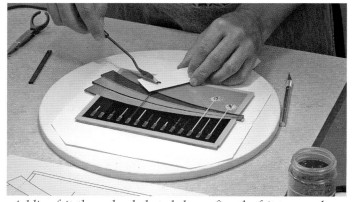

Adding frit through a hole to help confine the frit to one place

Isaac's Comet Tray

I started by placing thin resist paper on a shelf then positioned the clear base and support tabs. I cleaned and placed the 2nd layer design pieces, grinding to fit where necessary (using my Fusing bit) then secured this layer with glue. Then I added the design layer starting with the dichroic on clear noodles. I trimmed 14 pieces 1/2" - 13 mm long, then spaced them near the bottom of the black glass. Stringers of various colors and lengths were placed above the dichroic pieces. I dropped 3 piles of medium yellow & red frit by cutting a hole in a piece of paper to use as a stencil. I used liquid fusing glue to secure all design pieces. The assembly was placed in the kiln, the controller set for an **FS3 - Texture Fuse** schedule then I turned it on.

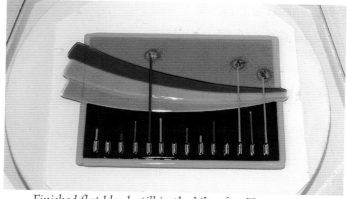

Finished flat blank still in the kiln after Texture Fuse

FS3 - Texture Fuse Schedule

Segment Description	Segment Number	Ramp Rate Degree Per Hour	Final Target Temperature	Hold-Soak Minutes
Primary Heat & Bubble Soak	1	500°F - 275°C	1150°F - 635°C	30
Intention Heat & Target Soak	2	300°F - 165°C	1330°F - 720°C	10
Rapid Drop to Anneal Soak	3	AFAP Full or 9999	950°F - 510°C	45
Slow Descent Anneal Cool	4	125°F - 67°C	700°F - 370°C	0
Power-off Cool to Room Temp	5	0000 Kiln Off	75°F - 25°C Room Temp	Do Not Open Kiln

Making the rounded corners on the fiber paper mold

To create the fiber paper mold I cut 2 pieces of 1/8" - 3 mm thick fiber paper, 10" x 7" - 26 x 18 cm then stacked them. I traced the outline of my flat blank then measured and drew a 3/4" - 2 cm inside border, ignoring the comet extensions. I used a grinder bit as a template to draw a radius on all 4 corners (about 1" - 2.5 cm in diameter). Then I used a craft knife to cutout this rounded corner rectangle. I removed the fiber paper cutout pieces then placed the double-thick fiber paper frame on a prepared kiln shelf. I centered the fused blank on the mold using the outside trace lines that I'd created earlier. Now all I have to do is place the assembly in the kiln, set the controller for an **MF1 - Mold Forming** schedule and fire it up.

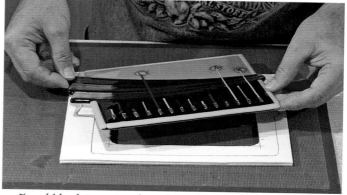

Fused blank is centered on the mold ready for slump firing

MF1 - Mold Forming Schedule

Segment Description	Segment Number	Ramp Rate Degree Per Hour	Final Target Temperature	Hold-Soak Minutes
Primary Heat & Bubble Soak	1	360°F - 195°C	1000°F - 540°C	10
Intention Heat & Target Soak	2	300°F - 165°C	1260°F - 682°C	10
Rapid Drop to Anneal Soak	3	AFAP Full or 9999	950°F - 510°C	45
Slow Descent Anneal Cool	4	125°F - 67°C	700°F - 370°C	0
Power-off Cool to Room Temp	5	0000 Kiln Off	75°F - 25°C Room Temp	Do Not Open Kiln

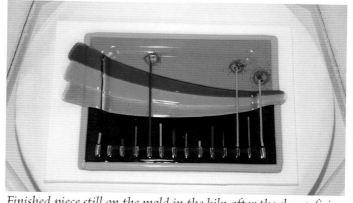

Finished piece still on the mold in the kiln after the slump firing

Such a Side Dish

Project at a Glance

Finished Project Size:
- 4 1/4" x 8 1/4" x 3/8"
  - 11 x 21 x 1 cm

Mold: Fiber Paper 1/8" - 3 mm
- 1 pc 10" square - 26 cm square

Kiln Firings: 1 Only
- FS4 - Contour Fuse

Glass & Components:
- Base Layer: smooth clear
- 2nd Layer: lt blue & celery green opal, lt blue, lt green cathedral, clear ribbed (irid & dichro)
- Design Layer: spaghetti stringers (asstd colors), powdered frit

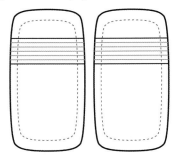

I wanted to design a couple of down-to-earth hors d'oeuvre dishes but I wanted to make them both in the same kiln load and I wanted to fuse and slump them in a single firing. Such a dish!

I printed out 2 paper copies of the twin-plate pattern drawing (you can download the drawing for free from www.joyoffusing.com). I placed one of the printouts on top of the 10" - 26 cm square fiber paper (1/8" - 3 mm thick) then used a craft knife to follow along the dashed line (not the outside perimeter line) and cut through both the paper drawing and the fiber paper below to create a twin cavity fiber paper mold. Then I placed a sheet of thin resist paper on my kiln shelf and centered the fiber paper mold on the resist paper.

Follow the template dash lines to cut the fiber paper mold

Cut the fibroid glass so it can be placed texture side up

Place & center the clear base layer on the fiber paper mold

Such a Side Dish Project 14

I cut my glass pattern templates from the 2nd paper printout. I cut around the outside perimeter on one of the dish drawings to use as the pattern for the base clear glass. Then I cut the other dish drawing into the 3 glass components that I'll need for the 2nd layer.

I started my pre-fuse assembly by tracing and cutting the 2 base layers from smooth clear glass. Then I cleaned and centered them on the fiber paper mold. It is important to make sure that these base glass pieces are not touching.

I then cut the 2nd layer components by tracing and scoring the various colors and textures of glass that I had selected. I cleaned these glass components then began the assembly by placing the 2 larger pieces on the base glass. I decided I wanted to give the clear center sections a little something extra. For the blue dish I covered the ribbed side with powdered blue frit then brushed the excess off with a sponge paintbrush. For the green dish I decided to use a piece of dichroic on clear ribbed glass and did not put the powdered frit on that piece. I finished positioning the rest of the pieces on the 2nd layer then strategically spread 6 colored stringers equally across the channels of the ribbed glass.

The final step was to put the kiln shelf with the glass assembly into the kiln. I had to decide on the best fusing schedule to achieve a flat fuse and a shape forming in a single firing. I reviewed my fusing level sample tiles and chose the **FS4 - Contour Fuse** schedule. I figured this schedule would provide an almost flat surface and would certainly be hot enough to slump into the fiber paper mold.

The primary ramp rate is relatively fast because the largest single piece is the base glass at 4 1/4" x 8 1/4" (35 SqIn) - 11 x 21 cm (231 SqCm). The ramp rate chart on page 23 suggests a surface area up to 42 SqIn - 325 SqCm can safely ramp at 600°F - 325°C, DPH.

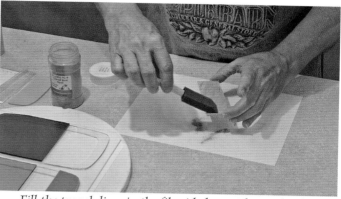

Fill the trough lines in the fibroid glass with powder frit

Accent a few fibroid lines with colorful spaghetti stringers

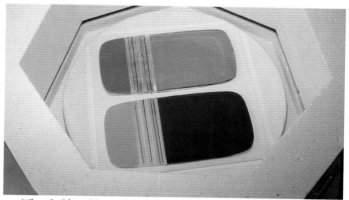

The shelf mold & glass are ready for the fuse/slump firing

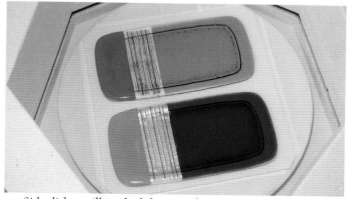

Side dishes still in the kiln - one firing from start to finish

FS4 - Contour Fuse Schedule

Segment Description	Segment Number	Ramp Rate Degree Per Hour	Final Target Temperature	Hold-Soak Minutes
Primary Heat & Bubble Soak	1	600°F -325°C	1150°F - 635°C	30
Intention Heat & Target Soak	2	300°F -165°C	1370°F - 745°C	10
Rapid Drop to Anneal Soak	3	AFAP Full or 9999	950°F - 510°C	45
Slow Descent Anneal Cool	4	125°F - 67°C	700°F - 370°C	0
Power-off Cool to Room Temp	5	0000 Kiln Off	75°F - 25°C Room Temp	Do Not Open Kiln

Blue Footed Vase

Project at a Glance

Finished Project Size:
- 7" dia x 3 1/2" - 17.5 dia x 9 cm

Mold: Ceramic, ring type
- Top: 7 1/2" - 19 cm dia, ring opening: 3" - 8 cm dia, height (including risers): 3 1/2" - 9 cm

Kiln Firings: 2 Total
- FS5 - Full Fuse
- MF1 - Drop Slump

Glass & Components:
- Base Layer: smooth clear
- 2nd Layer: clear, black & blue opal
- Design Layer: pattern dichroic on black, black spaghetti stringers

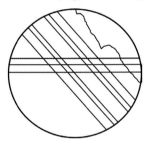

I am constantly researching new ways to shape and finish fused glass. I am excited to present this imaginative sculptural process that merges fused glass charisma with blown glass sophistication.

The fused blank for this project needs to be a full 2 layers thick to enable it to drop and stretch through the ring while maintaining an adequately thick wall. The base layer for the blank is a 7" - 18 cm clear circle. The 2nd layer consists of 3 blue opal strips, 2 narrow black strips, a raw factory edge from a black sheet and 2 pieces of clear, cut and shaped to fit on either side of the blue and black strips. The design layer is 3 pieces of patterned dichroic on black and a few black stringers on a diagonal. The blank assembly was placed on a prepared kiln shelf. Now I needed to create the foot disk. I carefully measured the drop ring opening and

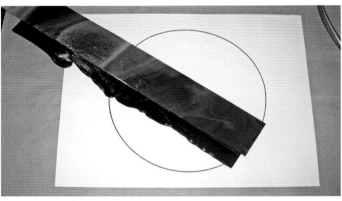

Design decisions, I wanted to use the unfinished glass edge

Assembly begins with blue & black strips and pre-fused dichro

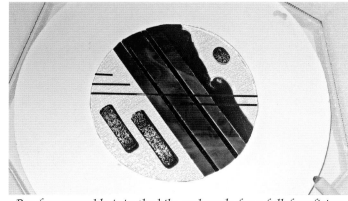

Pre-fuse assembly is in the kiln and ready for a full-fuse firing

Blue Footed Vase

found it to be 3" - 8 cm diameter so I cut 2 clear disks that were 1/4" - 6 mm smaller than the drop opening, at 2 3/4" - 7 mm diameter. These disks were stacked and placed on the kiln shelf beside the blank assembly. The shelf was placed in the kiln and fired to **FS5 - Full Fuse** schedule.

FS5 - Full Fuse Schedule				
Segment Description	Segment Number	Ramp Rate Degree Per Hour	Final Target Temperature	Hold-Soak Minutes
Primary Heat & Bubble Soak	1	500°F - 275°C	1150°F - 635°C	30
Intention Heat & Target Soak	2	300°F - 165°C	1425°F - 775°C	10
Rapid Drop to Anneal Soak	3	AFAP Full or 9999	950°F - 510°C	45
Slow Descent Anneal Cool	4	125°F - 67°C	700°F - 370°C	0
Power-off Cool to Room Temp	5	0000 Kiln Off	75°F - 25°C Room Temp	Do Not Open Kiln

The set up for the drop slump is straightforward. First make sure the fused foot disk passes easily through the opening in the drop ring mold, grind to fit if necessary. Then I place a piece of thin resist paper in the middle of the kiln shelf. Then I put a 2" - 5 cm disk of fiber paper (1/8" - 3 mm thick) on the shelf and center the foot disk over the fiber paper. Now place 3 kiln risers on the shelf and adjust them to fit under the drop ring mold. Now I look straight down through the opening to make sure the foot disk is centered directly below and adjust by moving the thin resist paper as necessary. Then I center the flat blank on the drop ring mold and place the entire assembly in the kiln.

Believe it or not I use the standard **MF1 - Mold Forming** schedule. The only modification for this drop slump is a longer soak time at the target temperature. After conducting a number of tests I found a 30 minute soak was perfect. At 20 minutes the drop had not quite touched the foot at 40 minutes the drop has spread to almost cover the foot. You will need to conduct testing of your own but keep good log records and your efforts will be rewarded.

DF1 - Drop Forming Schedule				
Segment Description	Segment Number	Ramp Rate Degree Per Hour	Final Target Temperature	Hold-Soak Minutes
Primary Heat & Bubble Soak	1	360°F - 195°C	1000°F - 540°C	10
Intention Heat & Target Soak	2	300°F - 165°C	1260°F - 682°C	30
Rapid Drop to Anneal Soak	3	AFAP Full or 9999	950°F - 510°C	45
Slow Descent Anneal Cool	4	125°F - 67°C	700°F - 370°C	0
Power-off Cool to Room Temp	5	0000 Kiln Off	75°F - 25°C Room Temp	Do Not Open Kiln

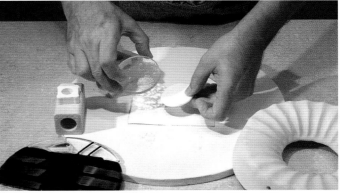

Glass disk for foot is placed on a smaller disk of fiber paper

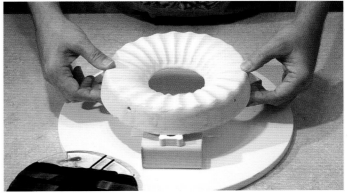

Drop mold is placed on risers & centered over the foot disk

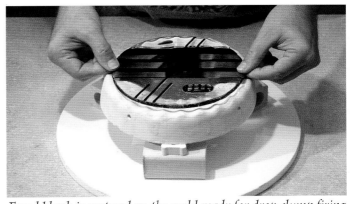

Fused blank is centered on the mold ready for drop-slump firing

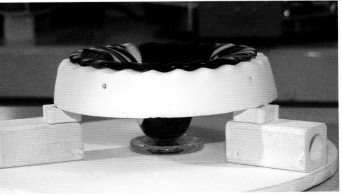

Finished piece still on the mold after the drop-slump firing

Jewelry Romanticized

Jewelry and glass have been in a close personal relationship for more than 5000 years. Glass beads are believed to be the earliest human-made glass objects with discoveries in Mesopotamia and Egypt dated to 3500 BC. Glass for personal adornment was a prized commodity, available only to the privileged for thousands of years. Today anyone with access to a glass fusing studio and some creative imagination can produce impressive glass jewelry pieces. Almost invariably the first project that new fusers make is a pendant, a brooch or earrings. These pieces require very little material and very little time. Someone with no glass working experience can make a breathtaking art piece on their very first try. Just imagine what they could do with a little fusing experience!

Project A – Layered and Tack Fused Jewelry Technique

Dichroic elements tacked fused to clear

Hearts of Mine Pendant

I cut the asymmetrical heart shape from thin smooth (1/16" - 1.6 mm) clear glass then refined the edge with an extra fine fusing bit on my grinder. Next I cut a very narrow strip of dichroic on clear and divided it into small squares that I placed around the perimeter. I found a tiny piece of thin red cathedral in my scrap drawer and used the pin-bit on my grinder to shape a tiny heart for the upper right center. I fired it using the FS1 - Elevated Tack schedule (see page 93). The last step was to glue a necklace bale to the backside.

Actual Size Drawing

Project B – Fused then Shaped and Fire Polished Jewelry Technique

Fused then shaped with a diamond saw

Twister Pendant

Fabrication starts with a small rectangle of thin (1/16" - 1.6 mm) black glass. I placed 3 randomly shaped pieces of patterned dichroic on the black glass, capped it with a piece of thin clear glass, and fired it to an FS5 - Full Fuse schedule (see page 93). I used my diamond ring saw to cut the jagged shapes around the perimeter and drilled a hole at the top for the bail. I put it back into the kiln to fire polish (use FS2 - pg 93). Then I created my own bail using silver wire (find wire wrapping instructions in our book 'Innovative Adornments' by Jayne Persico).

Actual Size Drawing

Jewelry Romanticized

ProTip: Drilling a Hole

Use a variable speed rotary tool with a 1/32" - 1 mm diamond pin bit. Place the pendant in a small dish and cover with water. Gently press the drill bit to the glass and hold steady until the hole is drilled.

Fused & Drilled Jewelry Technique - Project C

Fencepost Earrings

To create these earrings I cut 2 strips of thin clear and 2 strips dichroic on clear 3/16" x 2 1/2" - 5 x 64 mm then stacked them. I added a dichroic triangle and rectangle to the stacks. I placed them in my kiln and fired it to an FS2 - Dimensional Tack schedule (see page 93). Then I drilled a 5/64" - 2 mm hole in the top of each earring. I threaded a length of gold wire through the hole, added a small glass bead, and created a double wrapped loop to attach the earring loops. For detailed wire wrapping instructions see our book 'Innovative Adornments' by Jayne Persico.

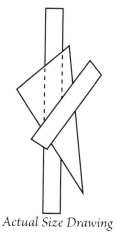

Actual Size Drawing

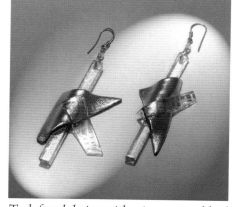

Tack fused design with wire wrapped bail

Wire Wrapping & Embellishment Jewelry Technique - Project D

Double Triangle Brooch

I made 2 identical shapes using a triangle of ripple dichroic for the base layer, a triangle of thin clear on top and then a smaller triangle of dichroic on black. These 2 triangles were placed in the kiln and fired it to an FS2 - Dimensional Tack schedule (see page 93). I drilled 2 holes in each piece and wired them together using a traditional double wrapped loop (with a small glass bead in the middle). Finally I used HoneyDoo Zuper Glue to attach 2 cultured pearls to the top of each piece and a brooch pin to the back.

Actual Size Drawing

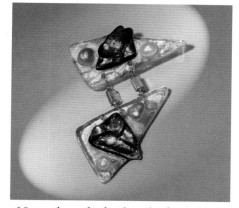

Natural pearls glued to the final design

Cast and Kiln Formed Jewelry Technique - Project E

Twin Flowers Bracelet

You will find many different casting molds that can be used for jewelry. This elegant bracelet was made by first casting a flat bracelet blank in a Colour de Verre mold using clear frit and thin pieces of clear dichroic glass. After it was fired I put it back in the kiln to bend it on my bracelet mold. Making bracelets this way is a lot of fun and very rewarding. You can learn more about creating fabulous jewelry pieces using these unique processes in 'Kiln Formed Bracelets' and 'Glass Kiln Casting' by Jayne Persico.

Shape Example

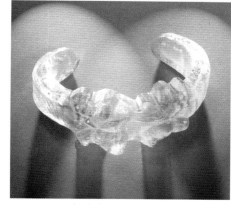

Casing with dichroic frit and clear glass

Pandichro's Box

Project at a Glance

Finished Project Size:
- 6 1/2" x 2 7/8" x 1 5/8" high
  - 16.5 x 7.5 x 4 cm high

Mold: Ceramic, casting type
- Box Lid: 4 1/4" x 7" x 1"
  - 11 x 18 x 2.5 cm
- Box Base: 5" x 7 3/4" x 2"
  - 13 x 20 x 5 cm

Kiln Firings: 2 total
- CS1 - Casting (x 2)

Glass: Casting shards
- Lid: 6.5 oz - 185 g total
- Base: 13.5 oz - 380g total

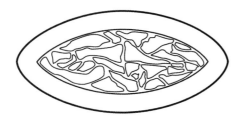

If you read the 'Succinct History of Glass' on page 5 (thanks to those who did) you'd know that glass casting has been around since 1500 BC. This box provides an opportunity to recreate history.

The good people at Colour de Verre create a wide variety of reusable ceramic molds for glass casting. The instructions they provide with every mold are excellent and there is no need to recreate them here. Be sure to read and follow their recommendations for resist coating, fill weights, and firing schedules.

I have used many of their smaller decorative molds for items such as flowers, sea life, jewelry, etc. but the designs I enjoy most are the boxes and the candleholders. I like my castings to have a transparent look that I get when I fill the molds with glass shards rather than frit. Here's how I created Pandichro's Box.

Spray CDV casting mold using MR-97 boron nitride release

Use mosaic nippers to break scrap glass into casting shards

Place CDV mold on a weigh scale then fill with casting shards

Pandichro's Box Project 17

This 'scrap casting' technique provides a welcome opportunity to use some leftover fusing glass. I score and break some scrap pieces into random narrow strips then use my mosaic nippers and a catcher box to break those down into glass shards about 1/2" - 15 mm or smaller (see photo on previous page). I keep the various colors and clear in separate containers.

When I'm ready to create a casting I throw a few handfuls of shards (separate colors) into my washtub to soak, agitate and dry. Then I place the prepared base mold on my digital scale and zero the tare weight. I place the shards into the mold cavity carefully, to avoid scratching the glass resist. I use a high ratio of clear to color (85 to 90% clear) to achieve my transparent look. I also prefer to use light cathedral colors but opals work nicely for some applications. When the mold is almost to the fill weight I begin to pile the shards up in the center of the mold to help reduce spikes & points.

To create the lid I used some scrap dichroic on black glass. I placed the pieces dichroic-side down to fill the oval space that is inside the lid mold. This oval is actually there to create the interlocking tab that holds the lid on the base but I'm going to use it to confine my dichroic design, while creating a clear border around the lid. After strategic placement of the dichroic glass I completed the fill with clear glass shards only. Both casting molds were placed into the kiln at the same time and fired to **CS1 - Casting** schedule.

Place both the base mold and the lid mold into the kiln

Cast firing is complete, notice the black back of the dichro

2nd firing of the lid to encapsulate the dichro in clear

CS1 - Casting Schedule				
Segment Description	Segment Number	Ramp Rate Degree Per Hour	Final Target Temperature	Hold-Soak Minutes
Primary Heat & Bubble Soak	1	300°F - 165°C	1250°F - 675°C	30
Intention Heat & Target Soak	2	300°F - 165°C	1430°F - 777°C	30
Rapid Drop to Anneal Soak	3	AFAP Full or 9999	950°F - 510°C	90
Slow Descent Anneal Cool	4	100°F - 53°C	600°F - 315°C	0
Power-off Cool to Room Temp	5	0000 Kiln Off	75°F - 25°C Room Temp	Do Not Open Kiln

For the final step, I flipped the lid over in the mold then added a clear oval-shaped cap to cover the dichroic section. I placed the mold back in the kiln to re-cast the lid and encapsulate the dichroic in clear using the same schedule as the original casting. By the way, don't waste the space in your kiln by re-firing this lid by itself. Fill another Colour de Verre mold - a candleholder perhaps or cut and assemble a flat fused project that can use the same final target point.

Finished box; dichro in lid is shiny bright and base is satin finish

Candles in the Wind

Project at a Glance

Finished Project Size:
- 5" diameter x 1 1/4" high
  - 13 cm diameter x 32 mm high

Mold: Ceramic, casting type
- Base: 7 1/2" dia x 2 3/4" high
  - 19 cm diameter x 7 cm high
- Plug: 1 1/2" dia x 2 1/2" high
  - 4 cm dia x 6.5 cm high

Kiln Firings: 1 only
- CS1 - Casting

Glass: Casting shards
- 18 oz - 500 g total

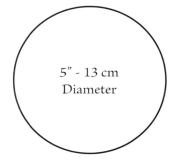

5" - 13 cm
Diameter

These tea light candleholders generate an interesting sensory contradiction. They appear to be light and airy but when they're picked up they present a surprising heft. An exquisite dilemma.

These candleholders were cast in a Colour de Verre reusable ceramic mold. I urge you to read and follow the excellent instructions the manufacturer provides, especially the recommendations for resist coating, optimum fill weights and firing schedules.

I am aware that most fusers fill these casting molds with pre-crushed glass frit. However frit cast pieces tend to be a little too opaque for my liking. I prefer a more transparent 'light and airy' appearance - more 'glass-like' if you will. That's precisely the effect I get when I fill these molds with scrap casting shards that I make myself.

'Scrap casting' has 2 advantages; the light and airy appearance that I just mentioned and the opportunity to use my leftover fusing glass. I free-hand score and break my scrap pieces into random width strips then use my mosaic nippers and a catcher box to break those down into glass shards about 1/2" - 15 mm, more or less (see photos on page 68). Sometimes I'll make a big batch of shards and store each color in separate containers (marked with the COE number).

I am hooked on the 'point and spray' convenience of MR-97 resist. The instructions tell you to use a stiff nylon kitchen brush to remove any pre-fired resist

Suspend the plug assembly & zero the tare weight

Fill the mold with color & clear shards using correct fill weights

Candles in the Wind

then recoat the mold before each use. I discovered this cleaning is really important, if you skip over this step you could find a permanent coating of MR-97 on the outside of your castings.

This mold comes with a ceramic plug that must be suspended in the center of the mold to create the cavity for the candle. The instructions suggest wrapping the plug with 1/16" - 1.6 mm thick fiber paper so it can be removed from the cast glass. The 1st time I made one of these I only had 1/8" - 3 mm fiber paper so I used that and it worked perfectly (this makes the cavity slightly larger).

When the mold is ready I place it on my digital scale and zero the tare weight. I place the shards in the mold a few at a time to avoid scratching the MR-97 resist. I always use a high ratio of clear glass to color to achieve my transparent look. As I'm approaching the recommended fill weight I begin to pile the glass shards up in the center and away from the sides, this helps to reduce spikes & flares.

When the mold is filled I place it in my kiln and fire it according to the **CS1 - Casting** schedule.

Mold is filled and has been placed in the kiln ready to go

The candleholder after firing; the edges are nicely rounded

CS1 - Casting Schedule				
Segment Description	Segment Number	Ramp Rate Degree Per Hour	Final Target Temperature	Hold-Soak Minutes
Primary Heat & Bubble Soak	1	300°F - 165°C	1250°F - 675°C	30
Intention Heat & Target Soak	2	300°F - 165°C	1430°F - 777°C	30
Rapid Drop to Anneal Soak	3	AFAP Full or 9999	950°F - 510°C	90
Slow Descent Anneal Cool	4	100°F - 53°C	600°F - 315°C	0
Power-off Cool to Room Temp	5	0000 Kiln Off	75°F - 25°C Room Temp	Do Not Open Kiln

The third photo at right shows the mold filled with a combination of clear glass shards along with purple and green coarse-size frit. The finished candleholder is at top-left in photo on the previous page. It has a very translucent look that I really like.

The last photo at right has the mold filled with clear glass shards and red opal mosaic-size frit. The finished candleholder is at center right in the photo on previous page. Notice how the larger pieces of red opal frit creates more separation between the clear and red chunks due to the opal quality of the red frit.

Both these molds were placed it in my kiln and fired according to the same **CS1 - Casting** schedule above.

Filled with clear shards plus purple and green coarse-size frit

Clear shards plus red opal mosaic-size frit (see photo page 70)

Crossroads Tray

Project at a Glance

Finished Project Size:
- 6 3/4" x 10 1/2" x 1"
  - 17 x 27 x 2.5 cm

Mold: Ceramic
- 7 1/2" x 12 1/2" - 19 x 30.5 cm
  rectangle, sushi style

Kiln Firings: 2 Total
- FS5 - Full Fuse
- MF1 - Mold Forming

Glass & Components:
- Base Layer: smooth clear
- 2nd Layer (all 1/16" thin glass):
  white opal plus asstd opal colors,
  some with iridized and dichroic

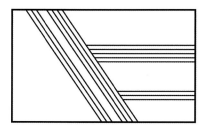

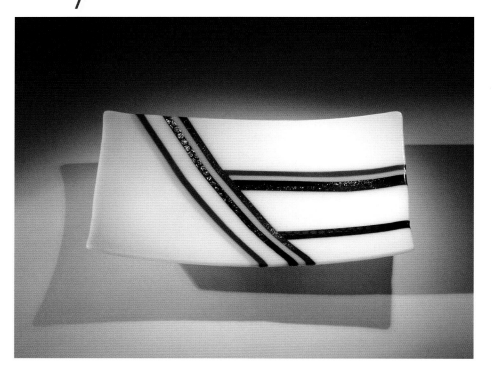

The narrow lines and linear graphic qualities of this project are greatly enhanced using this 'design fired down' technique that puts an emphasis on sharp clean images and straight lines.

The perfect prescription for a design with narrow parallel lines and high contrasting colors is this 'Design Fired Down' technique. Placing the design down will maintain straight lines with sharp crisp edges that a graphic design such as this one requires. In addition the dichroic and iridized surfaces are intensified when they are fired face down against the shelf.

The base layer for this project is standard thick 1/8" - 3 mm clear glass. The 2nd layer is thin fusing glass that is only 1/16" - 1.6 mm thick. Thin glass is extremely easy to cut and that makes it a great choice when creating a design like this with so many narrow strips.

Using the Portable Glass Shop to cut 1/4" - 6 mm strips

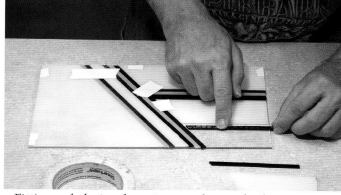

Fitting and placing the strips according to the design concept

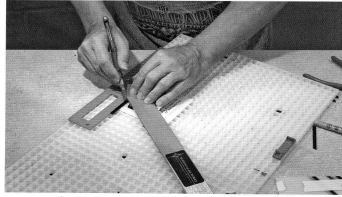

Using the jig system to score the angle on the end of a strip

Crossroads Tray Project 19

Since this project is all straight lines and angles it's a great opportunity to make good use of my portable glass shop. The first step was to cut a 7" x 11" - 18 x 28 cm clear rectangle for the base. Then I cut a piece of thin opal white the same size. I set up the strip cutter jig to make 1/4" - 6 mm strips then I cut two 10" - 25 cm strips from each of the 5 opal color selections.

Next I set the cutter guide to the pattern angle to cut the rest of the components. First I cut the larger white end piece and masking taped it to the base glass. Then I continued to trim and fit the colored strips and the white opal until the design was complete.

I placed a sheet of thin resist paper on my kiln shelf. Then I carefully turned the design over, one piece at a time, to rebuild it face side down on the shelf. Finally I placed the clear base glass on top of the design layer. I placed the assembly in the kiln and adjusted the design where necessary then set my controller to fire for an **FS5 - Full Fuse** schedule and turned the kiln on.

Cut & fit is finished, now the design is turned face down

The full-size clear cap is placed over the design, ready to fire

FS5 - Full Fuse Schedule

Segment Description	Segment Number	Ramp Rate Degree Per Hour	Final Target Temperature	Hold-Soak Minutes
Primary Heat & Bubble Soak	1	400°F - 220°C	1150°F - 635°C	30
Intention Heat & Target Soak	2	300°F - 165°C	1425°F - 775°C	10
Rapid Drop to Anneal Soak	3	AFAP Full or 9999	950°F - 510°C	45
Slow Descent Anneal Cool	4	125°F - 67°C	700°F - 370°C	0
Power-off Cool to Room Temp	5	0000 Kiln Off	75°F - 25°C Room Temp	Do Not Open Kiln

When the kiln had cooled I was very excited to see the result - it was exactly what I was hoping for. Now all I had to do was center it on the rectangle mold in the kiln then set my controller for an MF1 - Mold Forming schedule and fire it up.

Firing front side down, the lines are clean and very straight

MF1 - Mold Forming Schedule

Segment Description	Segment Number	Ramp Rate Degree Per Hour	Final Target Temperature	Hold-Soak Minutes
Primary Heat & Bubble Soak	1	340°F - 185°C	1000°F - 540°C	10
Intention Heat & Target Soak	2	300°F - 165°C	1260°F - 682°C	10
Rapid Drop to Anneal Soak	3	AFAP Full or 9999	950°F - 510°C	45
Slow Descent Anneal Cool	4	125°F - 67°C	700°F - 370°C	0
Power-off Cool to Room Temp	5	0000 Kiln Off	75°F - 25°C Room Temp	Do Not Open Kiln

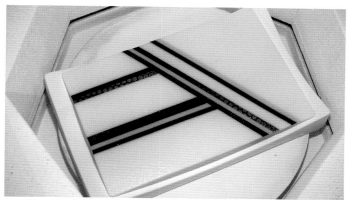
Flat blank placed on the mold ready for the slump firing

Project 20 Quadrant Plate

Project at a Glance

Finished Project Size:
- 9" square x 5/8" - 23 cm x 16 mm

Mold: Ceramic
- 9 1/4" - 24 cm square, dish style

Kiln Firings: 2 Total
- FS5 - Full Fuse
- MF1 - Mold Forming

Glass & Components:
- Base Layer: smooth clear
- 2nd Layer: black irid, white opal, spirit streaky plus assorted spaghetti & fettuccine noodles

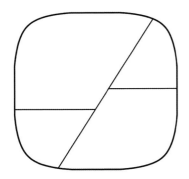

ridized surfaces (especially black iridized) are intensified when fired facedown. When you add parallel spaghetti stringers and diagonal bisecting lines, the best choice is 'design fired down'.

Paper template is cut and glass components are collected

It will be easier to cut the glass for this project if you create paper pattern templates to trace onto the glass. Make 2 copies of the pattern drawing (available for download on the book's website) then trim around the perimeter of one copy to use for the base glass template, and cut the other one into the quadrant pattern pieces.

I cut the clear base glass first then I cut the iridized black pieces (iridized side up), the white opal glass and the blue and white spirit streaky glass. Then I cleaned all 5 of these glass pieces.

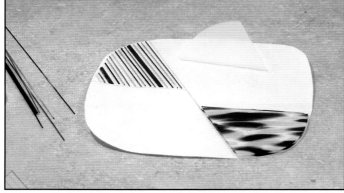

Stringers & noodles are cut and glued to the thin resist paper

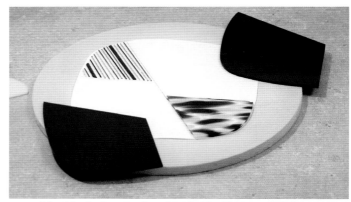

The black glass is placed irid side (design side) down

Quadrant Plate Project 20

Next I place the clear base on a piece of thin resist paper and trace the outline then I trim the paper to be 1/2" - 1 cm larger all around. Now I transfer the quadrant lines to the thin resist as well, to create an assembly drawing then placed this thin resist paper on my kiln shelf.

Now I can start the assembly. I position and trim my first spaghetti stringer and glued it to the thin resist paper. I trim and position the next stringer and glue it and continued this until all stringers have been placed and glued. Then I placed and glued the spirit glass and both of the iridized black pieces (iridized side down). Now I wait patiently until the glue is completely set (this is very important). Then I place and glue the white opal glass on top of the stringer assembly. The last piece to the puzzle is the clear glass to cover the entire assembly. I give this glue some time to set-up before moving the shelf assembly to the kiln. I set my controller for an FS5 - Full Fuse schedule and turned the kiln on.

The white is placed over the stringers then a clear glass piece

Assembly in the kiln, placed design down, for a full fuse firing

FS5 - Full Fuse Schedule

Segment Description	Segment Number	Ramp Rate Degree Per Hour	Final Target Temperature	Hold-Soak Minutes
Primary Heat & Bubble Soak	1	400°F - 220°C	1150°F - 635°C	30
Intention Heat & Target Soak	2	300°F - 165°C	1425°F - 775°C	10
Rapid Drop to Anneal Soak	3	AFAP Full or 9999	950°F - 510°C	45
Slow Descent Anneal Cool	4	125°F - 67°C	700°F - 370°C	0
Power-off Cool to Room Temp	5	0000 Kiln Off	75°F - 25°C Room Temp	Do Not Open Kiln

When the kiln had cooled I was thrilled to see that the stringers had not moved - they were still parallel! As a bonus the iridized surface on the black had intensified even more than I'd anticipated. Now all I had to do was put the mold in the kiln, center the glass on the mold and set my controller for an MF1 - Mold Forming schedule.

Turn the glass over, clean then place on the mold to slump

MF1 - Mold Forming Schedule

Segment Description	Segment Number	Ramp Rate Degree Per Hour	Final Target Temperature	Hold-Soak Minutes
Primary Heat & Bubble Soak	1	340°F - 185°C	1000°F - 540°C	10
Intention Heat & Target Soak	2	300°F - 165°C	1260°F - 682°C	10
Rapid Drop to Anneal Soak	3	AFAP Full or 9999	950°F - 510°C	45
Slow Descent Anneal Cool	4	125°F - 67°C	700°F - 370°C	0
Power-off Cool to Room Temp	5	0000 Kiln Off	75°F - 25°C Room Temp	Do Not Open Kiln

First look at the finished plate after the slump firing

French Bulldog Tile

Project at a Glance

Finished Project Size:
- 6" square - 15 cm square

Mold: Not Required
- Flat fired, mold not used

Kiln Firings: 2 Total
- FS1 - Elevated Tack
- FS5 - Full Fuse

Glass & Components:
- Base Layer: iridized red cathedral
- 2nd Layer: assorted dichroic on clear & black

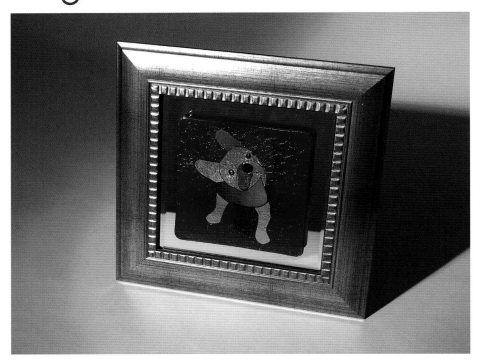

Puppies are so cute and I think this colorful little guy is going to muzzle his way into many hearts. 'Designs fired down' can make any portrait pop off the canvas.

I created this drawing from a photograph that friends gave me of their lovable French bulldog puppy. Creating a simplified line drawing from a photograph, any photograph (not just dogs), is not that difficult. The biggest hint I can give you is to leave out the troublesome details like the background and shadows then pay close attention to key features like the tilt of the head, placement of the eyes, location of the nose and ears or any other distinguishing feature. I was able to reduce this illustration to 12 pieces total, while effectively capturing Rocky's inquisitive personality.

Paper patterns are created to be traced onto the glass

Glass is cut according to the pattern tracing

Pieces are placed on the assembly drawing as they are created

French Bulldog Tile

It is absolutely necessary to have pattern templates and an assembly drawing for a portrait tile like this. I printed two copies of the drawing, one for the assembly and the other for the patterns. I cut a 6" - 15 cm square of iridized red cathedral for the background glass. Then I used various pieces of dichroic on clear and dichroic on black for the dog. Obviously I wasn't going for life-like colors since it's almost impossible to match those. It's far better to go completely in an unexpected direction and use crazy unreal colors.

After I had my pieces cut and shaped, I placed the assembly drawing under the iridized red cathedral and used the drawing lines as a guide to correctly position the cut pieces of glass. When everything was in place I used a little glue to secure them. I placed this tile in the kiln and fired it to an **FS1 - Elevated Tack** schedule.

The design is transferred and glued to the base glass

Design has been tack fired to the base glass

FS1 - Elevated Tack Schedule

Segment Description	Segment Number	Ramp Rate Degree Per Hour	Final Target Temperature	Hold-Soak Minutes
Primary Heat & Bubble Soak	1	350°F - 190°C	1150°F - 635°C	30
Intention Heat & Target Soak	2	300°F - 165°C	1245°F - 675°C	10
Rapid Drop to Anneal Soak	3	AFAP Full or 9999	950°F - 510°C	45
Slow Descent Anneal Cool	4	125°F - 67°C	700°F - 370°C	0
Power-off Cool to Room Temp	5	0000 Kiln Off	75°F - 25°C Room Temp	Do Not Open Kiln

I was actually very pleased with the tack fused portrait but I knew it would look even better after it had been fired 'design side down'. So I placed it back into the kiln, set my controller for an **FS5 - Full Fuse** schedule and turned the kiln on.

I was thrilled with the result. I used a little silicone to mount the tile to the surface of a mirror in a frame, then presented it to my friends as a gift (they loved it).

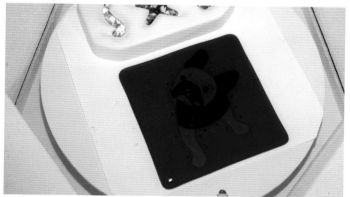

The tile is placed back into the kiln, design side down

First look at the finished tile after full fuse firing.

FS5 - Full Fuse Schedule

Segment Description	Segment Number	Ramp Rate Degree Per Hour	Final Target Temperature	Hold-Soak Minutes
Primary Heat & Bubble Soak	1	380°F - 205°C	1150°F - 635°C	30
Intention Heat & Target Soak	2	300°F - 165°C	1425°F - 775°C	10
Rapid Drop to Anneal Soak	3	AFAP Full or 9999	950°F - 510°C	45
Slow Descent Anneal Cool	4	125°F - 67°C	700°F - 370°C	0
Power-off Cool to Room Temp	5	0000 Kiln Off	75°F - 25°C Room Temp	Do Not Open Kiln

Petrofrit Platter

Project at a Glance

Finished Project Size:
- 9" square x 1 5/8" high
  - 23 cm square x 4 cm high

Mold: Ceramic
- 9 1/4" - 24 cm square sushi style

Kiln Firings: 3 Total
- FS3 - Texture Fuse
- FS5 - Full Fuse
- MF1 - Mold Forming

Glass & Components:
- Base Layer: black opal
- 2nd Layer: iridized red cathedral
- Design Layer: almond opal - fine frit, med amber - med frit

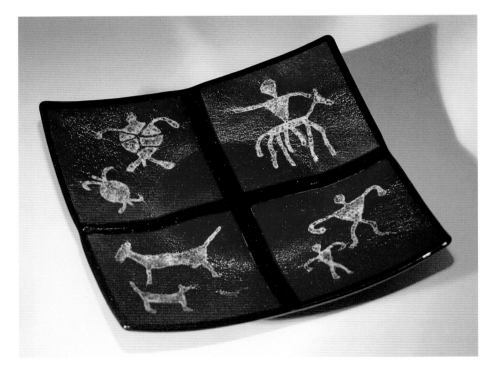

Petroglyphs have always fascinated me. They are ancient roadmaps, stories and family portraits painted by an artist. We are allowed to view them as a portfolio of work that is in the permanent collection of Mother Nature.

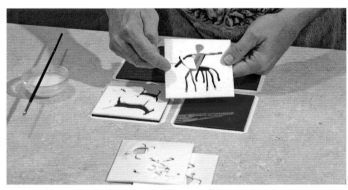

Petroglyph figures cut into 1/8" 3 mm fiber paper

This frit forming technique is really very simple to execute and it can be used to produce a very detailed image. I cut four 4" - 10 cm squares of iridized red cathedral for the petrofrit background. Then I used 1/8" - 3 mm thick fiber paper to create 4 stencil cutouts. I transferred the petroglyph drawings to the smooth side of the fiber paper (using tracing paper) then cut the stencil using a craft knife. I glued these stencil cutouts to the iridized side of the red glass then placed a sheet of thin resist paper under each square.

Glass laid irid side up and fiber paper is glued to top of glass

Fiber paper cutout is filled with a color mixture of frit

Petrofrit Platter

I filled the stencils using a mixture of almond and medium amber frit. I used an artist brush to remove the excess frit from the surface then placed all 4 tiles into my kiln and fired them to an **FS3 - Texture Fuse** schedule. I was able to use a fast ramp rate because the tiles are small (from the chart on page 23).

FS3 - Texture Fuse Schedule				
Segment Description	Segment Number	Ramp Rate Degree Per Hour	Final Target Temperature	Hold-Soak Minutes
Primary Heat & Bubble Soak	1	800°F - 435°C	1150°F - 635°C	30
Intention Heat & Target Soak	2	300°F - 165°C	1330°F - 720°C	10
Rapid Drop to Anneal Soak	3	AFAP Full or 9999	950°F - 510°C	45
Slow Descent Anneal Cool	4	125°F - 67°C	700°F - 370°C	0
Power-off Cool to Room Temp	5	0000 Kiln Off	75°F - 25°C Room Temp	Do Not Open Kiln

When the tiles had cooled I carefully removed the fiber paper stencils to reveal my petrofrit painting in 3-D. These tiles could be displayed just as they are but I think they look even better with the clean sharp edge that is produced by firing them 'design side down.'

I placed a sheet of thin resist paper on my kiln shelf then measured and drew some layout guidelines on it. I put the shelf in my kiln then placed the tiles facedown according to my layout lines. I then cut a 9" - 23 cm square of black glass (not iridized) and placed that on top of the petrofrit tiles. I now set my controller for an **FS5 - Full Fuse** schedule and turned the kiln on.

FS5 - Full Fuse Schedule				
Segment Description	Segment Number	Ramp Rate Degree Per Hour	Final Target Temperature	Hold-Soak Minutes
Primary Heat & Bubble Soak	1	340°F - 185°C	1150°F - 635°C	30
Intention Heat & Target Soak	2	300°F - 165°C	1425°F - 775°C	10
Rapid Drop to Anneal Soak	3	AFAP Full or 9999	950°F - 510°C	45
Slow Descent Anneal Cool	4	125°F - 67°C	700°F - 370°C	0
Power-off Cool to Room Temp	5	0000 Kiln Off	75°F - 25°C Room Temp	Do Not Open Kiln

The design side down, flat fused blank was stunning. I could have mounted it in a frame as is but I decided to slump it into my sushi style mold. I placed the blank on the mold, set my controller for a **MF1 - Mold Forming** schedule (use the MF1 schedule on page 93) with a 340°F - 185°C initial ramp rate. Then turned the kiln on to shape my platter.

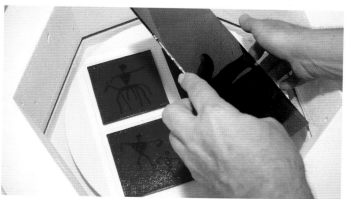

Tiles are placed on thin resist paper then fired to Texture Fuse

Fired tiles are cleaned then laid design side down

First look at full fused blank with petroglyph tiles

Finished platter piece after the slump firing

Wrong Way Charlie Tray

Frit Form Function Technique

Project at a Glance

Finished Project Size:
- 12" x 7" x 1"
  - 30 x 18 x 2.5 cm

Mold: Stainless Steel
- 12 1/2" x 8 1/2" - 32 x 22 cm oval

Kiln Firings: 3 Total
- SCS - Small Component Shaping
- FS5 - Full Fuse
- MF1 - Mold Forming

Glass & Components:
- Base Layer: blue cathedral & iridized thin clear
- Design Layer: powder & fine frits, mold formed seahorses

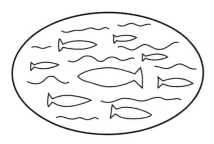

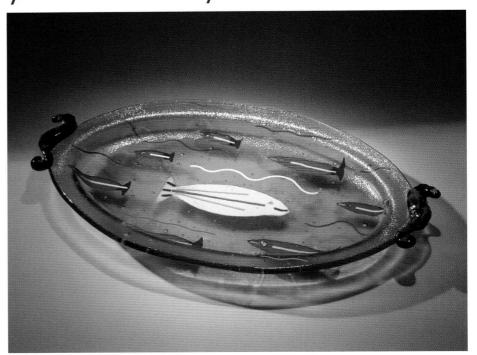

This project combines 5 fusing techniques into one interesting sculpture. It has frit stenciling, stringer shaping, design fired down, cast components, and slumping. Now where's my fishing pole?

Fiber paper with stencil cut outs is placed on a sheet of thin resist paper then filled with assorted powdered frit

I transferred the fish outlines to a piece of 1/8" - 3 mm thick fiber paper (using tracing paper) then cut the stencil using a craft knife. I placed a sheet of thin resist paper under the fiber paper and glued them together. I filled the stencils using some bright colors of powdered frit (they're tropical fish, so go wild). I used an artist brush to clear away some of the excess frit then I added a few stringers and dichroic eyes. I placed this frit assembly into the kiln and fired it using the **SCS - Small Component Shaping** schedule below. The fast ramp rate with no anneal soak means the fish will be cooked and ready in a few hours.

SCS - Small Component Shaping Schedule

Segment Description	Segment Number	Ramp Rate Degree Per Hour	Final Target Temperature	Hold-Soak Minutes
Intention Heat Target Soak	1	900°F - 495°C	1290°F - 700°C	10
Power-off Cool to Room Temp	2	0000 Kiln Off	75°F - 25°C Room Temp	Do Not Open Kiln

After the fish components have cooled off, I removed them one at a time from the fiber paper stencil. Some edges will be a little irregular with surplus frits and pieces. I like to clean these edges using my fusing bit on my grinder but be extra cautious, these fish are very thin and delicate and they break easily.

Stringers, dichroic and other details are added to top layer

Wrong Way Charlie Tray

Now I can begin the design assembly. I cut two ovals for the base layer, one from blue cathedral and the other from iridized thin clear. Next I place a sheet of thin resist paper on the kiln shelf then position and trace one of the ovals on the paper to be used as my layout guide. I arranged my fish facedown on the thin resist paper and then add some waveform shaped stringers. When I'm happy with the arrangement, I place the shelf with my fish and stringers in the kiln. I then position the clear oval, iridized side down, on top of my fish. I centered it with the oval layout line I drew earlier. I place the blue cathedral oval on top of the clear oval. I now set my controller for a **FS5 - Full Fuse** schedule and turned the kiln on.

Frit & fiber paper assembly ready for Dimensional Tack

FS5 - Full Fuse Schedule

Segment Description	Segment Number	Ramp Rate Degree Per Hour	Final Target Temperature	Hold-Soak Minutes
Primary Heat & Bubble Soak	1	300°F - 165°C	1150°F - 635°C	30
Intention Heat & Target Soak	2	300°F - 165°C	1425°F - 775°C	10
Rapid Drop to Anneal Soak	3	AFAP Full or 9999	950°F - 510°C	45
Slow Descent Anneal Cool	4	125°F - 67°C	700°F - 370°C	0
Power-off Cool to Room Temp	5	0000 Kiln Off	75°F - 25°C Room Temp	Do Not Open Kiln

I hate to fire a kiln with empty shelf space so very often I will throw something together quickly to fill up the shelf. One of those times I filled the space with a casting mold (2 seahorses & 1 starfish). Look behind the bulldog tile on page 77 and you'll see the sea creatures in the kiln. I didn't have a purpose for them at the time but after making this tray I had an idea to use the seahorse castings as tray handles.

Fish components arranged with shaped stringers & clear cap

I placed the fused blank on the stainless steel mold, design side up, then placed my seahorses to overlap the glass edge, making sure they were completely inside the perimeter of the mold. I set my controller for a **MF1 - Mold Forming** schedule, then fired it up.

Fused blank on the mold with seahorse castings for handles

MF1 - Mold Forming Schedule

Segment Description	Segment Number	Ramp Rate Degree Per Hour	Final Target Temperature	Hold-Soak Minutes
Primary Heat & Bubble Soak	1	360°F - 195°C	1000°F - 540°C	10
Intention Heat & Target Soak	2	300°F - 165°C	1260°F - 682°C	10
Rapid Drop to Anneal Soak	3	AFAP Full or 9999	950°F - 510°C	45
Slow Descent Anneal Cool	4	125°F - 67°C	700°F - 370°C	0
Power-off Cool to Room Temp	5	0000 Kiln Off	75°F - 25°C Room Temp	Do Not Open Kiln

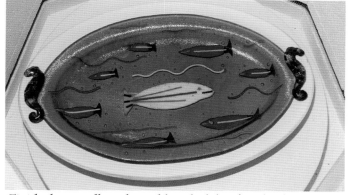

Finished tray still on the mold in the kiln after the slump firing

Project at a Glance

Finished Project Size:
- 8 1/2" diameter x 1 1/2" high
  - 22 cm diameter x 4 cm high

Mold: Ceramic
- 10 1/2" - 27 cm diameter round with 32 accordion pleats

Kiln Firings: 2 Total
- FS5 - Full Fuse
- MF1 - Mold Forming

Glass & Components:
- Base Layer: white opal
- 2nd Layer: iridized black, dichroic on clear, iridized clear coarse frit

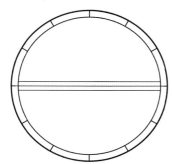

French Craquel antique glass (it's French spelling, that's why) is one of my favorite art glass textures. When iridized clear coarse frit is used to fill the background it creates a similar craquel effect.

Base glass disk is cut using a white opal

I was shooting for a blown glass look for this bowl so I decided to use the iridized clear coarse frit to give me the crackle look for the body of the bowl. I also wanted to create a glassblowing effect known as a 'lip wrap'. A contrasting color of molten glass is wrapped around the opening of the vessel, then when the vessel is opened to form the bowl shape, that contrasting color will be on the rim (or lip) of the bowl. To achieve this effect in fusing I needed to have a very narrow perimeter border. I decided to use iridized black for maximum contrast and make the black border pieces only 3/8" - 1 cm wide.

The irid black border pieces are placed and secured with glue

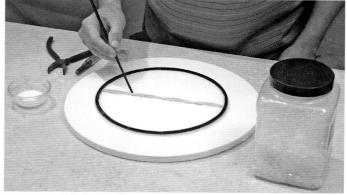
A row of dichroic glass is placed across the center and glued

Craquel Bowl Project 24

I created the full-size pattern template with 12 border segments. That makes each border piece approximately 2" long x 3/8" wide - 5 cm x 1 cm and that size is relatively easy to trace and cut with a glasscutter.

Once I had my border pieces finished, I cut the white opal base disk 8 1/2" diameter - 23 cm. I placed a sheet of thin resist paper on the kiln shelf then centered the white disk on the paper. Then I placed my border pieces around the top edge and secured them with a little fusing glue. Next I added two narrow rows of silver-green dichroic on clear 7 3/4" x 1/4" strips down the middle, just to add a little interest. Then I filled the background with the iridized clear coarse frit until it was piled slightly higher than the border glass. I used a small artist brush to sweep all loose frit off the black border and also off the kiln shelf. I placed the shelf assembly into the kiln then set my controller for an **FS5 - Full Fuse** schedule with a primary ramp rate of 400°F - 220°C per hour taken from the ramp rate chart on page 23. When everything was set I turned the kiln on.

A thick layer of clear irid course frit is added then leveled out

Pre-fire assembly in kiln ready for Contour Fuse firing

FS5 - Full Fuse Schedule

Segment Description	Segment Number	Ramp Rate Degree Per Hour	Final Target Temperature	Hold-Soak Minutes
Primary Heat & Bubble Soak	1	400°F - 220°C	1150°F - 635°C	30
Intention Heat & Target Soak	2	300°F - 165°C	1425°F - 775°C	10
Rapid Drop to Anneal Soak	3	AFAP Full or 9999	950°F - 510°C	45
Slow Descent Anneal Cool	4	125°F - 67°C	700°F - 370°C	0
Power-off Cool to Room Temp	5	0000 Kiln Off	75°F - 25°C Room Temp	Do Not Open Kiln

I was very pleased with the iridized black lip-wrap and the crackle background. I could hardly wait to see what it would look like once it had been shaped into a bowl. I set my controller for an **MF1 - Mold Forming** schedule then fired up the kiln.

Fused blank is centered on the mold ready for slump firing

MF1 - Mold Forming Schedule

Segment Description	Segment Number	Ramp Rate Degree Per Hour	Final Target Temperature	Hold-Soak Minutes
Primary Heat & Bubble Soak	1	340°F - 185°C	1000°F - 540°C	10
Intention Heat & Target Soak	2	300°F - 165°C	1260°F - 682°C	10
Rapid Drop to Anneal Soak	3	AFAP Full or 9999	950°F- 510°C	45
Slow Descent Anneal Cool	4	125°F - 67°C	700°F - 370°C	0
Power-off Cool to Room Temp	5	0000 Kiln Off	75°F - 25°C Room Temp	Do Not Open Kiln

Finished piece still on the mold in the kiln after the slump firing

Tutorial - Glass Fritage

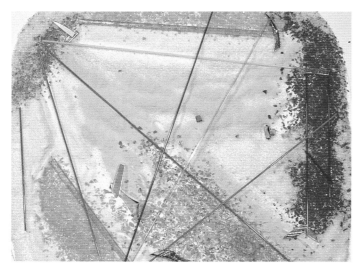

This is a typical unconfined Fritage assembly prior to firing

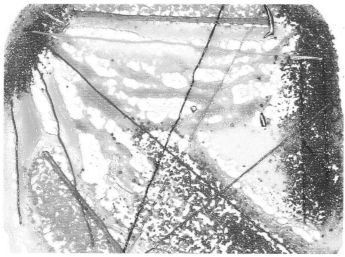

This is the same layout section as above after it was fired to a Fritage Development level of 1360°F - 738°C with no soak.

In the early 1900's Pablo Picasso coined the term 'Collage' (from coller, 'to stick') to express his new work that was "a glued assemblage of different forms to create a new whole". Découpage (from découper, 'to cut out'), the name given to another art form that involved cutting and placing images and pictures into an artwork. We also have works of 'Photomontage', 'Soundcollage', and now I'd like to introduce you to glass 'Fritage'. A term I use to describe "the assemblage of frit, stringers, noodles and other bits of glass with the intent to fashion a unique work of glass design.

I would hazard a guess to say that most fusers have placed frit and various chunks of glass on a kiln shelf to create frit balls and other shapes to use in future designs. I have seen some fabulous work using the process of 'Fritography' to create detailed scenes and life-like portraits. No doubt there are thousands of other unidentified examples of freeform glass works using frits, threads, chunks, noodles, bits, fragments, you name it. That's because these materials are amazingly versatile to work with. That's why I used them to fabricate the glass Fritage designs that I will describe for you in this tutorial section.

Glass desperately wants to be 1/4" - 6 mm thick. That's why a single layer of glass pulls up as it reaches fuse temperature and it's also why a 2 layer full fused tile relaxes to create a smooth surface with straight edges and rounded corners. The technique of Fritage uses this truth of physics to an advantage (see Hot Glass, Surface Tension, and Viscosity on page 22).

This is a framed Fritage assembly in progress. Notice how the frit and stringers are touching the frame to form a connection

Framed Fritage after it was fired to Contour Fuse level of 1370°F - 745°C with a 10 minute soak

These piles of frit powder will gather together to build a bunch of little rounded communities. A chunk of noodle will ball up and join with a stringer or pieces of frit to create another oddly shaped gang. Take a close look and compare the images on the previous page and you will discover that a seemingly solid layer of yellow, almond or red frit will shrivel and congeal into a leaner, more structured group. Pay particular attention to the way the stringers act like rafters and beams to connect several smaller groups - that is a key characteristic to keep in mind when you're designing a Fritage layout.

The other variable is the hold time. The yellow-red Fritage (previous page left) was fired to the standard Fritage Development schedule with no hold time while the green Fritage (right) was held for 10 minutes, increasing the size of the negative spaces.

The real mystery happens after the composition has been fused and the connected assembly is carefully lifted to reveal the parts and pieces that didn't stick with the group. These holes and spaces are the most unique and distinctive feature of the Fritage technique. Examine the design in the 'Framed Fritage' example (previous page, bottom) and take particular notice of the unusual gaps & spaces that wind around and between the glass clusters. Notice how this negative space enables the glass clusters to exist. These curious shapes cannot be produced any other way.

The question is, how can we use these unique properties to our creative advantage? I must admit I have only just begun to explore the potential. I have just enough space left in this book to introduce three exciting possibilities.

The first example is an unconfined assemblage that was FS1 - Elevated Tacked to a single layer of clear glass then slumped into a mold (page 86). The next piece is a constraint assembly where the Fritage components are arranged within a glass frame that ultimately becomes an integral part of the work (page 88). The 3rd example is a loose-knit composition that was left on the shelf undisturbed after the development firing. Then a single layer of clear glass was placed on top and fired to an FS4 - Contour Fuse. This created a decorative sheet that could have been cut and shaped for inclusion in other projects or the sheet can be used as it is and mold formed to create a shaped vessel (page 90).

I am confident you are going to enjoy exploring this engaging format and you will discover new and interesting ways to exploit this technique to create captivating artworks.

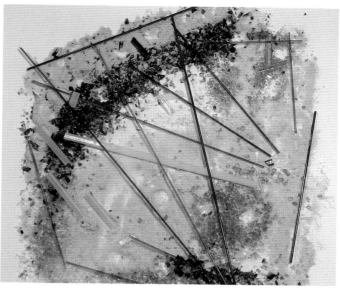

Assorted frits & stringers arranged on thin resist paper

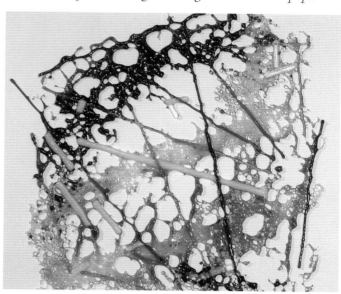

The unconfined Fritage assembly after it was fired

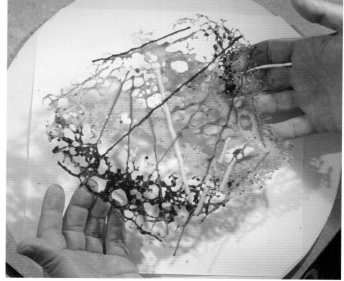

It is very delicate but it can be picked up for placement

Blue Plate Special

Project at a Glance

Finished Project Size:
- 8" diameter x 3/4"
  - 20 cm diameter x 2 cm

Mold: Ceramic
- 8 1/2" diameter - 22 cm diameter
  stylized triangle plate

Kiln Firings: 3 Total
- FDS - Fritage Development
- FS4 - Contour Fuse
- MF1 - Mold Forming

Glass & Components:
- Base Layer: smooth clear
- 2nd Layer: Fritage - assorted blue
  frits 1 powder, 1 fine & 2 medium;
  assorted stringers & noodles

The plate is topped with a lavishly textured Fritage composition. The surface is too rough to be used as a serving plate but the visual and tactile stimulation compensates for that shortcoming.

To make this unconfined Fritage, I placed a sheet of thin resist paper on my kiln shelf then spread some dark blue, medium sized frit by pouring it directly from the bottle. Then I spread around some light blue, fine sized frit. The idea is to create some thick areas and thin areas, sometimes concentrating the colors and other times making small heaps here & there. I continue to build my assemblage by adding another shade of medium and a powder. Then I placed some stringers and noodles to encourage the formation of an interconnecting web. Then I put it in my kiln and fired it to an **FDS - Fritage Development** schedule.

Freeform Fritage is scattered on a sheet of thin resist paper

Stringers, noodles & dichro bits are added for eye-appeal

The layout is placed in the kiln and fired to Contour Fuse level

Blue Plate Special Project 25

FDS - Fritage Development Schedule				
Segment Description	Segment Number	Ramp Rate Degree Per Hour	Final Target Temperature	Hold-Soak Minutes
Intention Heat Target Soak	1	900°F - 495°C	1360°F - 738°C	0
Power-off Cool to Room Temp	2	0000 Kiln Off	75°F - 25°C Room Temp	Do Not Open Kiln

The fused assembly is removed by turning it onto a clear disk

A Fritage fires quickly and is ready to go in a few hours. I removed the shelf with my fired piece still on it then placed a clear disk over it. Holding the clear disk securely I turned the shelf upside down transferring the Fritage to the disk. Then I placed the disk on some risers to make it easier to remove my fingers. The next step is to place my rounded triangle clear base (shaped for the plate mold) over the assembly and flip it over again, transferring the Fritage to my base glass - now with the correct side facing up. Then a little clean up around the edges and perhaps move or replace any loose groupings. Once I'm happy with the arrangement I put it back in my kiln and fire it to an **FS4 - Contour Fuse** schedule with a fast primary ramp rate of 500°F - 275°C per hour taken from the ramp rate chart on page 23.

The shaped base is placed and the Fritage is turned onto it

FS4 - Contour Fuse Schedule				
Segment Description	Segment Number	Ramp Rate Degree Per Hour	Final Target Temperature	Hold-Soak Minutes
Primary Heat & Bubble Soak	1	500°F - 275°C	1150°F - 635°C	30
Intention Heat & Target Soak	2	300°F - 165°C	1370°F - 745°C	10
Rapid Drop to Anneal Soak	3	AFAP Full or 9999	950°F - 510°C	45
Slow Descent Anneal Cool	4	125°F - 67°C	700°F - 370°C	0
Power-off Cool to Room Temp	5	0000 Kiln Off	75°F - 25°C Room Temp	Do Not Open Kiln

The flat blank looked great. The rounded triangle shape was made specifically for a ceramic plate mold that I have, so I placed the blank on that mold, put it in my kiln then set my controller for the **MF1 - Mold Forming** schedule below and fired the kiln.

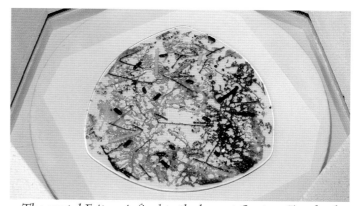

The crystal Fritage is fired to the base at Contour Fuse level

MF1 - Mold Forming Schedule				
Segment Description	Segment Number	Ramp Rate Degree Per Hour	Final Target Temperature	Hold-Soak Minutes
Primary Heat & Bubble Soak	1	360°F - 195°C	1000°F - 540°C	10
Intention Heat & Target Soak	2	300°F - 165°C	1260°F - 682°C	10
Rapid Drop to Anneal Soak	3	AFAP Full or 9999	950°F - 510°C	45
Slow Descent Anneal Cool	4	125°F - 67°C	700°F - 370°C	0
Power-off Cool to Room Temp	5	0000 Kiln Off	75°F - 25°C Room Temp	Do Not Open Kiln

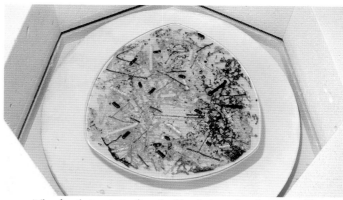

The final step is to fire the blank into the slump mold

Aurora Napkin Holder

Project at a Glance

Finished Project Size:
- 6 1/2" wide x 6" high x 2 1/2"
  - 16.5 wide x 15 high x 6.5 cm

Mold: Not Required
- Flat fired, mold not used

Kiln Firings: 3 Total
- FDS - Fritage Development
- FS4 - Contour Fuse
- MF1 - Mold Forming

Glass & Components:
- Base Layer: smooth clear
- 2nd Layer: borders - olive green & sky blue cathedral; Fritage - assorted green, yellow & blue frits, 1 powder, 2 fine & 2 med, stringers & noodles

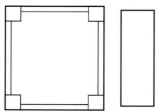

This common household device is transformed with the splendor of the Aurora Borealis, an effect produced using the glass Fritage technique. Two-part epoxy holds it all together.

Narrow strips of cathedral form a border for the Fritage layout

After Contour Fuse the frame Fritage is fused to a clear base

I put a sheet of thin resist paper on my kiln shelf then positioned 4 pieces of olive green cathedral, 1/4" wide x 6" long - 6 mm x 15 cm to make the frame. I then created the Fritage assembly by spreading 5 different frit varieties along with 3 colors of spaghetti stringers arranged diagonally, plus some dichroic noodles. I placed 4 sky-blue 3/4" - 2 cm squares to connect the corners and to provide an area for the Fritage to attach. I placed the assembly in my kiln and fired it to an **FDS - Fritage Development** schedule.

FDS - Fritage Development Schedule				
Segment Description	Segment Number	Ramp Rate Degree Per Hour	Final Target Temperature	Hold-Soak Minutes
Intention Heat Target Soak	1	900°F - 495°C	1360°F - 738°C	0
Power-off Cool to Room Temp	2	0000 Kiln Off	75°F - 25°C Room Temp	Do Not Open Kiln

Next I cut a clear base glass 6 1/2" x 6" - 16.5 x 15 cm then placed my Fritage frame on top. I loaded this new assembly into my kiln and fired it to an **FS4 - Contour Fuse** schedule.

I needed to create the tile for the backside of the napkin holder. I cut the clear base and frame strips exactly the same size and colors that I used for the front tile. I then cut a clear and blue piece for the floor.

Aurora Napkin Holder

I assembled the base and frame on my kiln shelf then added a simple dichroic border design. The floor piece is 2" x 6" - 5 x 15 cm and has a clear base with a sky-blue top. I put both components into my kiln and fired them to the **FS4 - Contour Fuse** Schedule.

FS4 - Contour Fuse Schedule

Segment Description	Segment Number	Ramp Rate Degree Per Hour	Final Target Temperature	Hold-Soak Minutes
Primary Heat & Bubble Soak	1	400°F - 220°C	1150°F - 635°C	30
Intention Heat & Target Soak	2	300°F - 165°C	1370°F - 745°C	10
Rapid Drop to Anneal Soak	3	AFAP Full or 9999	950°F - 510°C	45
Slow Descent Anneal Cool	4	125°F - 67°C	700°F - 370°C	0
Power-off Cool to Room Temp	5	0000 Kiln Off	75°F - 25°C Room Temp	Do Not Open Kiln

The napkin holder back panel and floor are also Contour Fused

Now I'll fabricate the napkin holder using masking tape and 2-part epoxy (the longer curing epoxy is much better than the fast cure variety). Silicone and E6000 adhesives will not work.

I grind both side edges of the floor piece (not the ends) to make them straight and square. Then I cut a piece of corrugated cardboard slightly smaller than the glass and tape it to the bottom (tape the ends only). This cardboard will force the floor piece to be raised slightly off the holder's lower edge.

The final step is to cold fuse (epoxy) the 3 components together

Next I cut another strip of corrugated cardboard 2" wide x 8" long - 5 x 20 cm, bend it to form a triangle, and tape the ends together. I place this cardboard triangle between the front and back tiles to hold them exactly 2" - 5 cm apart. Then secure this assembly with masking tape (see photo 2nd from top).

Now I mix the epoxy to glue the floor piece to the sides. I squeeze about 2" - 5 cm from each tube of the epoxy compound then use a toothpick to mix them together thoroughly. I spread a generous amount of mixed epoxy along both edges of the floor piece (the same area I ground earlier) then place it cardboard side down on my bench. I carefully pick up the taped together sides and hold them directly over the floor piece. I spread the lower edge open slightly then lower the assembly until the bottom edge touches the bench. Then I squeeze them together (see 3rd photo) until the epoxy oozes out along the edges. I check the floor and sides to make sure they are square then I apply plenty of tape to hold the sides together securely.

Corrugated cardboard spacers are created for the epoxy build

Now leave it alone for at least 12 hours then remove the tape and fill it with dinner napkins.

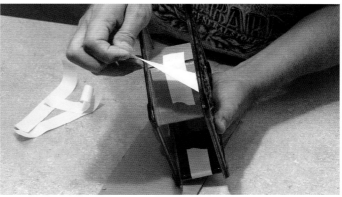

After the epoxy has set the cardboard spacers are removed

Watercolor Bowl

Project at a Glance

Finished Project Size:
- 10" diameter x 1 1/2" high
  - 25.5 cm diameter x 4 cm high

Mold: Ceramic
- 10 1/2" - 27 cm diameter
  round with 32 accordion pleats

Kiln Firings: 3 Total
- FDS - Fritage Development
- FS4 - Contour Fuse
- MF1 - Mold Forming

Glass & Components:
- Base Layer: smooth clear
- Design Layer: Fritage - assorted
  blue frits 1 powder, 1 fine & 1
  medium, stringers & noodles

10" - 25.5 cm
Diameter

The Fritage design on this bowl reminds me of watercolor splatter painting. It's only one layer of glass with smooth top surface (the design is on the bottom) making it a very light and useful dish.

Spreading frit, stringers & noodles on a thin resist paper

I call this style of Fritage a loose-knit composition because the components are wildly scattered and sparsely connected. My intention was to fuse this Fritage to the bottom side of a 10" - 25.5 cm diameter clear disk. I was fascinated by the possibility of creating my own custom art glass sheet that I could cut and shape to make components for an entirely new fuse piece. With that in mind I placed a sheet of thin resist paper on my kiln shelf and used a pencil to trace the outline of my 10" - 25.5 cm diameter disk onto the resist paper.

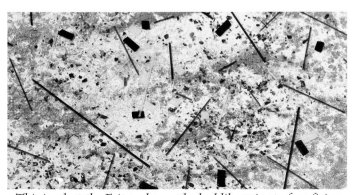

This is what the Fritage layout looked like prior to fuse firing

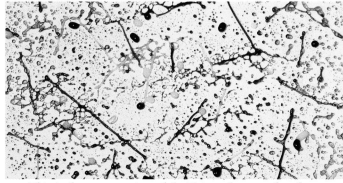

This is the same section of the Fritage layout after firing

Watercolor Bowl

I began by distributing the medium sized frit in a very uniform pattern. Then I spread the fine frit around, leaving some areas with concentrated amounts and others with none at all. I sprinkled the powdered frit primarily around the perimeter of my circle with a few splashes across the center. The stringers were kept relatively short and I tried to lay them down in a very random way. I broke the noodles into very short bits (less than 1/2" - 1 cm) so they would form into large dots. Then I used a narrow paintbrush to sweep any scattered bits of glass back into the circle. I put it into my kiln then ran an **FDS - Fritage Development** schedule.

The Fritage is undisturbed on the shelf after firing

FDS - Fritage Development Schedule

Segment Description	Segment Number	Ramp Rate Degree Per Hour	Final Target Temperature	Hold-Soak Minutes
Intention Heat Target Soak	1	900°F - 495°C	1360°F - 738°C	0
Power-off Cool to Room Temp	2	0000 Kiln Off	75°F - 25°C Room Temp	Do Not Open Kiln

When the kiln had cooled I placed my 10" - 25.5 cm diameter clear disk on top of the Fritage, being very careful that I did not disturb the delicate design. I set the controller to run an **FS4 - Contour Fuse** schedule.

A clear disk is placed over the assembly to be fused

FS4 - Contour Fuse Schedule

Segment Description	Segment Number	Ramp Rate Degree Per Hour	Final Target Temperature	Hold-Soak Minutes
Primary Heat & Bubble Soak	1	500°F - 275°C	1150°F - 635°C	30
Intention Heat & Target Soak	2	300°F - 165°C	1370°F - 745°C	10
Rapid Drop to Anneal Soak	3	AFAP Full or 9999	950°F - 510°C	45
Slow Descent Anneal Cool	4	125°F - 67°C	700°F - 370°C	0
Power-off Cool to Room Temp	5	0000 Kiln Off	75°F - 25°C Room Temp	Do Not Open Kiln

I was so impressed with this loose-knit composition disk that I decided it was strong enough to stand on its own, so I placed it on my pleated bowl mold and slumped it to a **MF1 - Mold Forming** schedule.

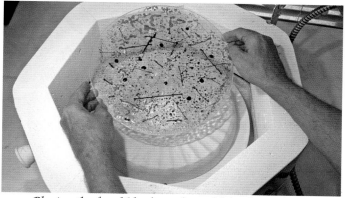

Placing the fused blank on the mold for slump firing

MF1 - Mold Forming Schedule

Segment Description	Segment Number	Ramp Rate Degree Per Hour	Final Target Temperature	Hold-Soak Minutes
Primary Heat & Bubble Soak	1	320°F - 175°C	1000°F - 540°C	10
Intention Heat & Target Soak	2	300°F - 165°C	1260°F - 682°C	10
Rapid Drop to Anneal Soak	3	AFAP Full or 9999	950°F - 510°C	45
Slow Descent Anneal Cool	4	125°F - 67°C	700°F - 370°C	0
Power-off Cool to Room Temp	5	0000 Kiln Off	75°F - 25°C Room Temp	Do Not Open Kiln

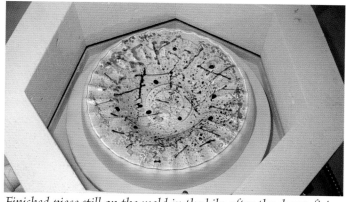

Finished piece still on the mold in the kiln after the slump firing

At a Glance - Fusing Levels

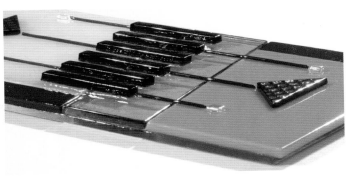

FS1 - Elevated Tack Schedule - 1245 °F - 675 °C

All glass components are firmly stuck together and the surface is shiny but the edges are only slightly blunted. The stringers and other elements are fully elevated and retain an undistorted shape.

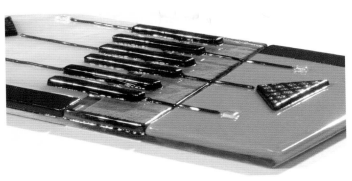

FS2 - Dimensional Tack Schedule - 1290 °F - 700 °C

The edges are rounding slightly and the surface is polished. The stringers are melting but still raised while the space between sections on the 2nd layer have opened up slightly to form an attractive channel.

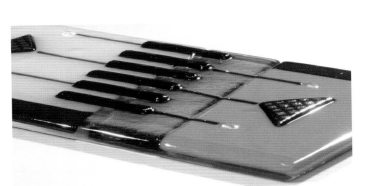

FS3 - Texture Fuse Schedule - 1330 °F - 720 °C

The top decoration layer retains a pronounced raised texture that is about 50% of the original thickness. The edges and corners are rounding off and the adjoining space between sections are beginning to fill in.

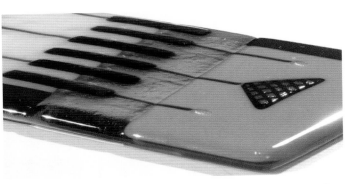

FS4 - Contour Fuse Schedule - 1370 °F - 745 °C

This firing is about 80% of the way to a full-fuse. The edges and corners are almost fully rounded off but the top surface still has a lot of texture that you can see and feel, while presenting a full fused effect.

FS5 - Full Fuse Schedule - 1425 °F - 775 °C

This firing is 97% flat - only the dichroic triangles are slightly raised. The corners and edges are completely rounded off but remain relatively straight and the surface is slick and shiny.

FS6 - Deep Fuse Schedule - 1470 °F - 800 °C

This tile is 100% flat. The only difference between this firing and the Full Fuse firing is the dichroic triangles are now flat. The thickness is the same and the overall effect is more or less the same.

FS1 - Elevated Tack Schedule

Segment Description	Segment Number	Ramp Rate Degree Per Hour	Final Target Temperature	Hold-Soak Minutes
Primary Heat & Bubble Soak	1	See Ramp Rate Chart	1150°F - 635°C	30
Intention Heat & Target Soak	2	300°F - 165°C	1245°F - 675°C	10
Rapid Drop to Anneal Soak	3	AFAP Full or 9999	950°F - 510°C	45
Slow Descent Anneal Cool	4	125°F - 67°C	700°F - 370°C	0
Power-off Cool to Room Temp	5	0000 Kiln Off	75°F - 25°C Room Temp	Do Not Open Kiln

FS2 - Dimensional Tack Schedule

Segment Description	Segment Number	Ramp Rate Degree Per Hour	Final Target Temperature	Hold-Soak Minutes
Primary Heat & Bubble Soak	1	See Ramp Rate Chart	1150°F - 635°C	30
Intention Heat & Target Soak	2	300°F - 165°C	1290°F - 700°C	10
Rapid Drop to Anneal Soak	3	AFAP Full or 9999	950°F - 510°C	45
Slow Descent Anneal Cool	4	125°F - 67°C	700°F - 370°C	0
Power-off Cool to Room Temp	5	0000 Kiln Off	75°F - 25°C Room Temp	Do Not Open Kiln

FS3 - Texture Fuse Schedule

Segment Description	Segment Number	Ramp Rate Degree Per Hour	Final Target Temperature	Hold-Soak Minutes
Primary Heat & Bubble Soak	1	See Ramp Rate Chart	1150°F - 635°C	30
Intention Heat & Target Soak	2	300°F - 165°C	1330°F - 720°C	10
Rapid Drop to Anneal Soak	3	AFAP Full or 9999	950°F - 510°C	45
Slow Descent Anneal Cool	4	125°F - 67°C	700°F - 370°C	0
Power-off Cool to Room Temp	5	0000 Kiln Off	75°F - 25°C Room Temp	Do Not Open Kiln

FS4 - Contour Fuse Schedule

Segment Description	Segment Number	Ramp Rate Degree Per Hour	Final Target Temperature	Hold-Soak Minutes
Primary Heat & Bubble Soak	1	See Ramp Rate Chart	1150°F - 635°C	30
Intention Heat & Target Soak	2	300°F - 165°C	1370°F - 745°C	10
Rapid Drop to Anneal Soak	3	AFAP Full or 9999	950°F - 510°C	45
Slow Descent Anneal Cool	4	125°F - 67°C	700°F - 370°C	0
Power-off Cool to Room Temp	5	0000 Kiln Off	75°F - 25°C Room Temp	Do Not Open Kiln

FS5 - Full Fuse Schedule

Segment Description	Segment Number	Ramp Rate Degree Per Hour	Final Target Temperature	Hold-Soak Minutes
Primary Heat & Bubble Soak	1	See Ramp Rate Chart	1150°F - 635°C	30
Intention Heat & Target Soak	2	300°F - 165°C	1425°F - 775°C	10
Rapid Drop to Anneal Soak	3	AFAP Full or 9999	950°F - 510°C	45
Slow Descent Anneal Cool	4	125°F - 67°C	700°F - 370°C	0
Power-off Cool to Room Temp	5	0000 Kiln Off	75°F - 25°C Room Temp	Do Not Open Kiln

FS6 - Deep Fuse Schedule

Segment Description	Segment Number	Ramp Rate Degree Per Hour	Final Target Temperature	Hold-Soak Minutes
Primary Heat & Bubble Soak	1	See Ramp Rate Chart	1150°F - 635°C	30
Intention Heat & Target Soak	2	300°F - 165°C	1470°F - 800°C	10
Rapid Drop to Anneal Soak	3	AFAP Full or 9999	950°F - 510°C	45
Slow Descent Anneal Cool	4	125°F - 67°C	700°F - 370°C	0
Power-off Cool to Room Temp	5	0000 Kiln Off	75°F - 25°C Room Temp	Do Not Open Kiln

MF1 - Mold Forming Schedule

Segment Description	Segment Number	Ramp Rate Degree Per Hour	Final Target Temperature	Hold-Soak Minutes
Primary Heat & Bubble Soak	1	See Ramp Rate Chart	1000°F - 540°C	10
Intention Heat & Target Soak	2	300°F - 165°C	1260°F - 682°C	10
Rapid Drop to Anneal Soak	3	AFAP Full or 9999	950°F - 510°C	45
Slow Descent Anneal Cool	4	125°F - 67°C	700°F - 370°C	0
Power-off Cool to Room Temp	5	0000 Kiln Off	75°F - 25°C Room Temp	Do Not Open Kiln

CS1 - Casting Schedule

Segment Description	Segment Number	Ramp Rate Degree Per Hour	Final Target Temperature	Hold-Soak Minutes
Primary Heat & Bubble Soak	1	300°F - 165°C	1250°F - 675°C	30
Intention Heat & Target Soak	2	300°F - 165°C	1430°F - 777°C	30
Rapid Drop to Anneal Soak	3	AFAP Full or 9999	950°F - 510°C	90
Slow Descent Anneal Cool	4	100°F - 53°C	600°F - 315°C	0
Power-off Cool to Room Temp	5	0000 Kiln Off	75°F - 25°C Room Temp	Do Not Open Kiln

SCS - Small Component Shaping Schedule

Segment Description	Segment Number	Ramp Rate Degree Per Hour	Final Target Temperature	Hold-Soak Minutes
Intention Heat Target Soak	1	900°F - 495°C	1245°F - 675°C	10
Power-off Cool to Room Temp	2	0000 Kiln Off	75°F - 25°C Room Temp	Do Not Open Kiln

FDS - Fritage Development Schedule

Segment Description	Segment Number	Ramp Rate Degree Per Hour	Final Target Temperature	Hold-Soak Minutes
Intention Heat Target Soak	1	900°F - 495°C	1360°F - 738°C	0
Power-off Cool to Room Temp	2	0000 Kiln Off	75°F - 25°C Room Temp	Do Not Open Kiln

Note: See Ramp Rate Chart on page 23 to determine the correct DPH for the Primary Heat

At a Glance - Molds We Used

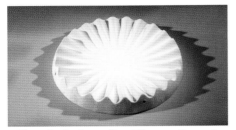

Plate Style Accordion Flutes - Ceramic
12 1/2" diameter - 32 cm diameter
Project 1 page 34 - Project 9 page 52

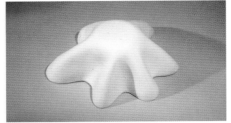

Bowl Style Drapery Flutes - Ceramic
12" diameter x 4" high- 30 cm x 10 cm
Project 2 page 35

Plate Style Oval - Stainless Steel
12 1/2" x 8 1/2" - 32 cm x 22 cm
Project 3 page 36 - Project 23 page 80

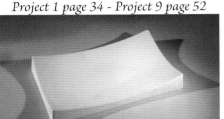

Sushi Style Rectangle - Ceramic
7 1/2" x 12 1/2" - 9 cm x 30.5 cm
Projects on pages 40, 44, 54, & 72

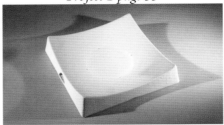

Sushi Style Large Square - Ceramic
9 1/4" square - 24 cm square
Projects on pages 42, 48, 50, 56, & 78

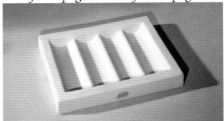

Wave Rectangle - Ceramic
8" x 10" - 20 cm x 25 cm
Project 7 page 48 - Project 8 page 50

Stringer Forming - Stainless Steel
8" x 3/4" - 20 cm x 2 cm
Project 9 page 52

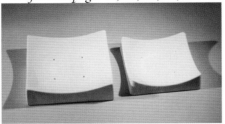

Sushi Style Small Square - Ceramic
6" & 5" square - 15 cm & 13 cm square
Project 10 page 54

Ring - Ceramic
7 1/2" diameter 3" center - 19 cm, 7 cm
Project 15 page 64

Colour de Verre Box - Ceramic
5" x 7 3/4"- 13 cm x 20 cm
Project 17 page 68

Colour de Verre Candleholder - Ceramic
7 1/2" diameter - 19 cm diameter
Project 18 page 70

Plate Style Square - Ceramic
9 1/4" square - 24 cm square
Project 20 page 74

Colour de Verre Seahorse - Ceramic
7" x 4" - 18 cm x 10 cm
Project 23 page 80

Bowl Style Round - Ceramic
10 1/2" diameter- 19 cm diameter
Project 24 page 82

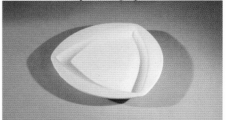

Stylized Triangle Plate - Ceramic
7 " triangle - 20 cm triangle
Project 25 page 86

Index

Wardell
PUBLICATIONS INC

Fusing & Kilnworking - Instruction and Projects

Stained Glass - Instruction, Projects and Inspiration

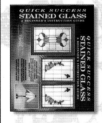   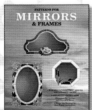    

    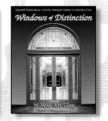  

e-mail: info@wardellpublications.com website: www.wardellpublications.com